T0393481

Palgrave Studies in Workplace Spirituality and Fulfillment

Series Editors

Satinder Dhiman, School of Business, Woodbury University, Burbank, CA, USA

Gary E. Roberts, Robertson School of Government, Regent University, Virginia Beach, VA, USA

Joanna Crossman, University of South Australia, Adelaide, SA, Australia

Satinder Dhiman, *Editor-in-Chief*
Gary Roberts and Joanna Crossman, *Associate Editors*

By way of primary go-to-platform, this Series precisely maps the terrain of the twin fields of *Workplace Spirituality and Fulfillment* in the disciplines of business, psychology, health care, education, and various other allied fields. It reclaims the sacredness of work—work that is mind-enriching, heart-fulfilling, soul-satisfying and financially-rewarding. It fills the gap in scholarship in the allied disciplines of Workplace Spirituality and Flourishing. Using a comprehensive schema, it invites contributions from foremost scholars and practitioners that reflect insightful research, practices, and latest trends on the theme of workplace spirituality and fulfillment. The uniqueness of this *Series* lies in its anchorage in the moral and spiritual dimension of various positive forms of leadership—such as Authentic Leadership, Servant Leadership, Transformational Leadership, and Values-Based Leadership.

We welcome research monographs and multi-authored edited volumes representing myriad thought-positions on topics such as: Past, Present and Future Directions in Workplace Spirituality; Workplace Spirituality and World Wisdom/Spiritual Traditions; Culture Studies and Workplace Spirituality; Spiritual, Social and Emotional intelligence; Nature of Work; Mindfulness at Work; Personal Fulfillment and Workplace Flourishing; Workplace Spirituality and Organizational Performance; Inner Identity, Interconnectedness, Community and Transcendence; Managing Spiritual and Religious Diversity at Work; Spirituality and World Peace Imperative; Sustainability and Spirituality; Spirituality and Creativity; and Applied Workplace Spirituality in Health Care, Education, Faith-based Organizations, et al.

More information about this series at
https://link.springer.com/bookseries/15746

Paresh Mishra · Suresh Kalagnanam

Managing by Dharma

Eternal Principles for Sustaining Profitability

Paresh Mishra
Purdue University Fort Wayne
Fort Wayne, IN, USA

Suresh Kalagnanam
Edwards School of Business
University of Saskatchewan
Saskatoon, SK, Canada

ISSN 2662-3668   ISSN 2662-3676 (electronic)
Palgrave Studies in Workplace Spirituality and Fulfillment
ISBN 978-3-030-90668-9   ISBN 978-3-030-90669-6 (eBook)
https://doi.org/10.1007/978-3-030-90669-6

This Palgrave Macmillan imprint is published by the registered company Springer Nature Switzerland AG
The registered company address is: Gewerbestrasse 11, 6330 Cham, Switzerland

Preface

The primary aim of this book is to marry the wisdom in ancient Hindu texts on dharma with the modern scientific research on management to identify a set of principles that can aid business organizations in sustaining profitability. The authors draw inspiration from several sources: (1) management is a curious combination of art and science, (2) leadership is complex and alternative models of leadership are critical to developing the field, and (3) knowledge is sacred and must be shared widely.

Change is the only constant in society, everything else is transitory in nature. That the world has witnessed tremendous change—technological, social, and environmental—over the past 40 years is an understatement at best. Technology has enabled global connectivity in ways that may have been unimaginable a mere twenty years ago. There is more awareness about climate change and the potential effects of the actions of individuals, communities, institutions, and organizations on the sanctity and longevity of the environment. Societal changes have led to increased awareness regarding basic human rights, inequities confronting society, and the importance of social responsibility. An important consequence, particularly for businesses, is the relative importance of potentially conflicting goals and objectives. These consequences have evoked different types of responses that may be both positive (e.g., a genuine focus on sustainability and social responsibility) and negative (e.g., fraudulent behavior, greenwashing).

The practice of management, in an ever-changing contextual environment, requires a holistic approach to steer the organization in the right direction and achieve its desired objectives in a responsible and respectful manner. Such an approach requires a delicate balancing act by taking into account the magnitude, scope and variety of objectives, stakeholder needs and economic, environmental and regulatory considerations. A critical question that emerges is whether changes can be made in a piece-meal manner or if a more fundamental transformation is required? This book proposes that when the pace of change in the business environment becomes rapid, a solid foundation to guide the organization is not just necessary but critical.

Every organization needs a steady foundation or an underlying set of principles that will guide the organization and the individuals within it. This book proposes that *dharma* provides such a foundation; it discusses the unique contributions that the *dharmic* tradition makes to the field of management. Within the Hindu tradition, *dharma* refers to a set of principles that nourishes, supports, and sustains the growth of the self, society, and the entire world. *Dharma* is sustainable thinking, and *dharmāchāra* refers to all those practices that promote sustainability. Specifically, we discuss the decentralized and open-source aspects of the *dharmic* tradition and their implications to practicing managers. We also describe how the ethical aspect of *dharma* is rooted in respectful pluralism, and thereby helps bridge secular ethics and spiritual ethics approaches to management.

How can any organization transition towards being *dharmic*? Is there a tangible destination or is it a continuous journey? Previous literature, depending upon the originating discipline, talks about people, processes, systems, and culture/climate. The chapter on enabling mechanisms identifies external factors, individual factors, and organizational factors as three broad categories. While external factors may catalyze change the remaining two categories—individual and organizational factors—are critical to enabling change. A key emphasis of this chapter is the explicit recognition that individual and organizational factors must be mutually reinforcing to result in meaningful change. Another classification of the enabling mechanisms is technical and humanistic systems. Humanistic systems must be the core around which organizations should develop the technical systems as support mechanisms, rather than the other way around. Regardless of how the enabling mechanisms are classified, leadership and the concepts of a learning organization assume critical importance and are discussed.

Change in any organization is not easily achievable due to a variety of hurdles, both internal and external to any organization, that become genuine impediments or convenient excuses to either stop changes or significantly reduce the pace of change. The key is to recognize the hurdles, accept them and find ways to move on (easier said than done). Interestingly some of the qualities underlying *dharma—Indriya Nigraha* (discipline of the body, mind, and senses), *Satyam* (truth), and *Dhriti* (determination)—can help overcome resistance to change. The book also includes three case studies, including one business and two community-based organizations, that illustrate the practice of dharma. The book offers some concluding thoughts for academics and practicing managers to contemplate upon.

Fort Wayne, USA

Saskatoon, Canada

Paresh Mishra

Suresh Kalagnanam

Acknowledgments

A project like this is impossible to complete without the help of many individuals along the way. First, we thank Marcus Ballenger for recognizing the value of such a project and giving us the opportunity to pursue it. Next, we thank Joanna Crossman, Satinder Dhiman, and Gary E. Roberts, editors of the series 'Palgrave Studies in Workplace Spirituality and Fulfillment' for their feedback on the proposal and the manuscript. Their comments greatly helped in improving the contents of this book. We then thank each of the individuals who were generous with their time in sharing their knowledge and expertise about the subject matter and their experiences in translating principles into practice. This book would have been incomplete without such rich data. We thank Nishit Gandhi for his research assistance. The role of the publisher's production team is extremely critical in ensuring that the final output is error-free; we thank them for their diligence. Finally, we thank our respective families for their constant encouragement and support throughout this project.

CONTENTS

List of Figures

CHAPTER 1

Need for a Steady Foundation

1.1 Vasistha's Curse

Vishnu, who is considered the supreme God within the Vaishnava tradition of Hinduism, has eight attendant deities known as Vasus. The literal meaning of the Sanskrit word, Vasu, is radiance, benevolent, or wealth giver. Once upon a time, the eight Vasus along with their respective wives decided to travel to Earth. After visiting many auspicious places, they reached the ashram (or hermitage) of Maharshi Vasistha (or the great sage, Vasistha). Unfortunately, Vasistha was not at the ashram then. So they wandered around the ashram and came across Vasistha's miraculous cow, Kāmadhenu, which had the power to provide anything that her owner desired. Legend also had it that anyone who drank Kāmadhenu's milk became immortal.

One of the Vasus was Prabhās. His wife got filled with greed when she saw Kāmadhenu and wanted to possess her. She told Prabhās that she wanted the divine cow for one of her girlfriends who was a mortal human being. The idea was to feed her friend with Kāmadhenu's milk so that they could enjoy each other's friendship forever.

Prabhās said they should not steal the cow because it was wrong to do so. Plus, the destiny of human beings was always decided by their deeds, and it would be wrong to interfere in this divine order. However, Prabhās' wife wouldn't listen and continued to coax him. The infatuated husband

P. Mishra and S. Kalagnanam, *Managing by Dharma*, Palgrave Studies in Workplace Spirituality and Fulfillment, https://doi.org/10.1007/978-3-030-90669-6_1

ultimately conceded, but under the condition that they would return the cow to Vasistha once his wife's friend had had the cow's milk. Prabhas discussed with the other seven Vasus to devise a plan of how to steal and return Kāmadhenu before Vasistha returned to his ashram.

However, Vasistha returned before they could steal. And with his divine powers also found out about the stealing plan that the Vasus had hatched. Appalled that gods (the Sanskrit equivalent of god is *Devatā*, meaning he who gives) could even entertain the thought of stealing, he cursed the Vasus to be born as humans. The Vasus realized their mistake and pleaded for forgiveness. So, the curse was lessened such that the seven Vasus who had planned to assist in the stealing would be liberated soon after their human birth. However, Prabhās being the prime mover of the theft plan would have to endure a long life on Earth. The curse on him would be slightly mitigated by the fact he would become one of the most esteemed persons of his time.

Because of this curse, the eight Vasus later took birth on Earth as children of goddess Ganga. As predicted, seven of them got immediate salvation after their birth, but one lived a long life and came to be known as Bhishma. Bhishma became one of the most powerful warriors and respected personalities in the Mahabharata. However, his life, and later even his death, was filled with immense suffering.

1.2   FROM RAGS TO RICHES AND BEYOND

We'll come back to Vasistha's Curse story a little later in the chapter but now let's switch to 1942 in rural Missouri. Ken was born that year. His parents used to own a small feed store, but it went out of business. His father doubled as a Baptist preacher in the area but that didn't bring home much money. So, the family sought refuge with some relatives and worked at their farm as laborers. For most of his childhood, Ken lived with his parents and two siblings in a ramshackle of a house that did not have indoor plumbing.

Ken took up adult responsibilities pretty early in life. He drove the tractor and plowed the field, while still a boy. The physical labor, however, did not bog Ken down. Instead, it increased his resolve to strive hard for success. It certainly helped that he was prodigiously smart. On completing high school, he earned a scholarship to study at the University of Missouri. The scholarship amount was not enough for all his expenses, but he managed to survive by doing odd jobs on the side. At the university, Ken found his passion for economics when he attended a class taught by a popular professor named Pinkney Walker. Economics inspired him so much that he took more courses in the subject, which helped him graduate with a Masters' degree in economics. A few years later, he even went on to get a Ph.D. degree in economics from the University of Houston.

Ken began his career as an economist for an oil company, but after a few years, he joined the US Navy, ahead of the Vietnam draft. He did well in the navy, rising to the rank of lieutenant within three years. But he moved out of the navy when his old mentor, Prof. Walker offered him a position in the Federal Power Commission.

Over the next several years, Ken worked in varied positions in different organizations. But wherever he worked, he succeeded in impressing everyone with his talents, work ethic, and pleasant disposition. Unsurprisingly, he moved up the corporate ladder swiftly and became one of the highest-paid executives of corporate America. There were perhaps many who envied Ken, but his niceness ensured that no one resented him.

In 1985, Ken founded his own company. It was a merger of two relatively small companies. Ken made sure that the new company was founded on the strength of strong positive values. He declared that his company stood for "Respect, Integrity, Communication and Excellence." The company's mission statement explicitly stated:

> We treat others as we would like to be treated ourselves. We do not tolerate abusive or disrespectful treatment. Ruthlessness, callousness and arrogance don't belong here.
>
> We work with customers and prospects openly, honestly and sincerely. When we say we will do something, we will do it; when we say we cannot or will not do something, then we won't do it.

Understanding the importance of congruence of values across the supply chain, the company instituted ethical policies for its important stakeholders, such as employees, contractors, and suppliers. The company's policy declared:

> Because we take our responsibilities to our fellow citizens seriously, we act decisively to ensure that all those with whom we do business understand our policies and standards.

> Compliance with the law and ethical standards are conditions of employment, and violations will result in disciplinary action, which may include termination.
>
> We "require [our] contractors, suppliers, and vendors to uphold the same respect for human rights that we require of ourselves…"

Ken's company went on to become one of the most admired companies in America. It was voted "America's Most Innovative Company" by Fortune magazine for six consecutive years from 1996 to 2001.

While being mightily successful in the corporate world, Ken did not forget his social responsibilities. He gave back generously to the community. He donated about 1% of his pre-tax earnings to various charitable causes. This included support in millions of dollars to organizations such as the United Way, Baptist church, Character Education Partnership, Aspen's Biochemical Research Foundation, a National League baseball team, among others.

Ken's story unquestionably resembles the epitome of how business ought to be conducted. However, as some of you might have already guessed, the Ken we are referring to here is the disgraced Kenneth Lay who found Enron (McLean & Elkind, 2013).

Enron had over 22,000 employees in 2000. Its revenue surpassed $100 billion the same year, but all this was a mirage. After it was revealed in 2001 that the company had been involved in deep financial fraud for years, it lost all its market capitalization. It was forced to file for Chapter 11 bankruptcy. The fraud resulted in losses exceeding $74 billion for its shareholders. Employees not only lost their jobs but also the money that they had put in their pension funds.

Ken was certainly not the only person responsible for Enron's collapse. Fraud at such a large scale does not happen without the complicity of many people. The company's CEO, Jeffrey Skilling, and COO, Andrew Fastow were other key players, among many others. Enron's collapse brought down another multi-billion dollar company, Arthur Andersen when it came under scrutiny for being the auditors of Enron. Arthur Andersen was one of the oldest and largest accounting firms in the world and had close to 28,000 employees before its demise.

How can a company that was started by a man with seemingly strong foundations gain the disrepute of being one of the largest corporate frauds in history? How could a company that ostensibly dotted all the 'i's and crossed all the 't's of corporate ethical conduct become the apotheosis of deceptions engaged by corporations? What could be done to minimize the chances of such terrible frauds happening in our society? In the real world, can business and ethics exist side-by-side as they do in the phrase "Business Ethics" or are they antithetical to each other?

1.3 THE PARADOX OF FRAUD

We may have a strong desire for simple explanations when it comes to unpleasant events. However, frauds, especially large-scale ones, do not ever have one single cause. For the Enron debacle also, scholars have provided numerous explanations, including but not limited to corrupt leadership (Eckhaus & Sheaffer, 2018; Gini, 2004; Johnson, 2003; Seeger & Ulmer, 2003), failure of corporate governance (Clark & Demirag, 2002; Heath & Norman, 2004; Vinten, 2002), toxic organizational culture (Knottnerus et al., 2006; Kulik, 2005; Wong, 2002), flaws in government regulations (Baker, 2003; Brown, 2005), failure of the accounting systems of checks and balances (Benston, 2006; Benston & Hartgraves, 2002; Bratton, 2003; Carnegie & Napier, 2010; Clarke, 2005), and the complex structure and information asymmetry within the industry which makes it is easy for unscrupulous individuals to deceive government and people (Arnold & De Lange, 2004; Heath & Norman, 2004; Schwarcz, 2004).

Based on some of the above explanations, businesses and governments have also implemented several reforms in the world of business and corporate governance (Markham, 2015; Ronen, 2014), although they haven't been completely effective. In 2001, Enron may have been the largest Chapter 11 bankruptcy in history, but there have been many other high profile corporate frauds in the post-Enron period, some of which have been many times larger than that of Enron's. Based on the parameter of asset value at the time of bankruptcy, Enron at $65 billion is now the seventh-largest Chapter 11 Bankruptcy in the USA (Hallman, 2019). The top six bankruptcies in this list—viz., Lehman Brothers at $691 billion, Washington Mutual at $328 billion, WorldCom at $104 billion, General Motors at $82 billion, CIT Group at $71 billion, and Pacific Gas and Electric Company at $71 billion—all happened in the post-Enron era.

We do not mean to imply that all bankruptcies are directly related to corporate fraud. Bankruptcies happen for many reasons (Ooghe & De Prijcker, 2008). However, in the above list of seven largest Chapter 11 bankruptcies, only one case—that of General Motors—was not overtly related to fraud. General Motors' Chapter 11 bankruptcy was a result of the general recession that followed the financial crisis of 2007–2008, which though was caused by fraudulent underwriting and predatory lending practices (Agarwal et al., 2014; Williams, 2010). Our point is just that the innumerable large-scale cases of corporate fraud and the corresponding fallout show that post-Enron reforms haven't been very effective in preventing such scams. Rather, it seems that we can try to minimize asymmetries and flaws within any complex system that encourages fraud, but they cannot ever be eliminated.

Dan Davies (2021), in his recent book, *Lying for Money: How Legendary Frauds Reveal the Workings of Our World*, provides an interesting insight. He describes four basic kinds of financial frauds (viz. Long Firm Fraud, Counterfeiting, Control Fraud, and Distributed Control Fraud). We will not go into the details of these types, but what is common to all of them is that somebody always breaks the trust that the transacting parties had bestowed in the business transactions. Wherever there is trust, there is always a possibility that the trust will be broken. The problem is that businesses cannot operate efficiently without there being a certain level of trust between the transacting partners and in the overall system. Even at the most basic level, transacting parties have to trust each other to pay invoices and deliver the promised goods. Not having that trust would mean doing all transactions on a cash-on-delivery basis, which is a highly inefficient way of conducting business, and thus undesirable to anyone who wants to scale up and expand one's business operations.

The trust equation also highlights another problem with corporate governance reforms. All reforms essentially try to install mechanisms within the system that would increase people's general trust that they would not be ripped off. If these reforms are reasonably successful, people do develop greater trust in the system. However, the increased trust causes them to reduce the thoroughness with which they earlier scrutinized every business transaction, which paradoxically increases the probability of them getting defrauded. Davies (2021) called this the Canadian Paradox to explain the extremely high prevalence of fraud in the Canadian financial sector despite it being a high-trust society where businesses are generally honest, and laws are fair and steadfastly enforced. In contrast, fraudsters find it difficult to operate in low-trust societies— where "political institutions are fragile and corrupt, business practices are dodgy, debts are rarely repaid and people, rightly, fear being ripped off on any transaction" (Davies, 2021)—because in such societies people tend to do the bigger business transactions within family relatives and close networks that may have centuries of shared history.

The key lesson from the Canadian paradox is that reforms targeting to improve the checks and balances within a system may, in an absurd way, may increase the probability of fraud within that system as it becomes easier for any unscrupulous person "to carry out a securities fraud in a market where dishonesty is the rare exception rather than the everyday rule" (Davies, 2021, p. 16). This certainly does not mean that we should do away with regulatory reforms, but it does imply that the net positive effect of regulatory reforms may not be substantial in the long run.

If system-level regulatory change isn't the panacea that people assume it to be, then what are the alternatives?

1.4   THE GLOOM OF GREED

Probably, one of the most frequently attributed causes of corporate frauds both in the academic literature and popular press—is greed (Dillon & Cannon, 2010; Lo et al., 2005; Partnoy, 2010; Swartz & Watkins, 2004; Toffler & Reingold, 2004; Wang & Murnighan, 2011; Wang et al., 2011). This literature asserts that the primal motivation of all famous defrauders, be it Charles Ponzi from the early 1900s or the more recent avatars such as Bernie Madoff, Kenneth Lay, and Jeffrey Skilling, has always been greed. Even when they are not explicitly breaking the law, greedy people, according to this literature, engage in high-risk behaviors to maximize personal benefits that often lead to huge losses and sometimes bankruptcies. A recent study that analyzed data from over 300 publicly traded companies from varied industries provided empirical confirmation to this premise (Takacs Haynes et al., 2017).

In 2002, the chairman of the Federal Reserve, Alan Greenspan, while testifying before a US Senate Committee said, "An infectious greed seemed to grip much of our business community" (Shapiro, 2021, p. 340). Greenspan's point was not that humans had suddenly become greedier than their ancestors. He asserted, "It is not that humans have become any more greedy than in generations past. It is that the avenues to express greed had grown so enormously" (Gates, 2002).

Greenspan used these statements to justify his proposed regulatory changes. One can certainly argue about the appropriateness of the specific changes instituted by Greenspan, but we are not against regulations per se. Regulations are necessary to keep the economic system fair and dependable, especially when there is a failure in the foundations of the free market economy. For example, regulations would be vital to limit monopoly power, anti-competitive behaviors, predatory pricing, or even the sale of extremely hazardous products. Our stand, as we have discussed in the previous section, is that regulations have their limitations and may not be sufficient to curb the dangers of greed.

Greenspan's statement also highlights a key aspect of greed: it has been with us from the time that humans have existed. Greed has been attributed to be the root cause of not just corporate fraud but also innumerable brutal atrocities in history. For example, Goldberg (1994) describes how greed—the primary motivator of the Spanish exploration of the new world—also led to horrifying barbarity against the native Americans. In one notable incident, the greedy explorers brutally murdered Atahualpa, the leader of the Incas even after he converted to Christianity and gave his captors billions of dollars worth of gold and silver in ransom. Goldberg explains how the Holocaust, apart from being a case of racial and religious hatred, was also an outcome and manifestation of "greed on an obscene scale" (p. 40).

Historical and contemporary examples of the perils of massive greed may lull us into the belief that we, common individuals are at no risk of its excesses. However, that would be a delusion. The grip of greed on common people's psyche can be observed from the numerous recorded incidents during the Black Friday sales in America, where on many occasions, average shoppers have turned exceedingly violent against co-shoppers and store employees just so that they can purchase some coveted product at a discount (Kaplan, 2020; Wheelwright, 2018; http://blackfridaydeathcount.com/). Similar reprehensible behaviors were also observed recently during the initial stage of the COVID-19 pandemic when few people in America and Canada created an artificial scarcity of hand sanitizer and toilet paper rolls by buying them in bulk from stores and then reselling them at ridiculously exorbitant prices to make some quick buck (David et al., 2021; Hains, 2020).

The dangers of greed are well documented. It is perhaps for this reason that most religions denounce it. For example, within the Christian tradition, greed is one of the seven deadly sins. Tickle (2004, p. 28) called it the "the mother of the Deadly Clan" because of how it impacts the other six sins (viz. pride, envy, sloth, gluttony, lust, and anger). Greed is also decried in Judaism because of how it prompts people to grab more than their share which "robs other people of their opportunity to get their due" (Bloch, 1984, p. 154) Oka and Kuijt (2014) explain that greed is frowned upon in Islam as well for going against the precept of moderation, although they also note that in the Quran and Hadiths there is the "divine encouragement of unlimited wealth accumulation" (p. 39).

In the Hindu tradition, the Bhagavad Gita (Verse 16.21) describes greed as one of the three gates—the other two being lust and anger—that lead to the hell of self-destruction (Gambhirananda, 1984). Ramayana, another one of the sacred texts of Hindus, (in the *Ayodhya Kanda*) illustrates how greed was one of the driving forces of queen Kaikeyi that led her to banish Sri Rama into fourteen years of exile in the forest (Venkatesananda, 1988). Kaikeyi was the stepmother of Rama and had always been very affectionate and caring towards him, but when she came under the grips of greed, she could not control herself from engaging in a series of actions that forced the legitimate and most capable inheritor of the throne to live in exile for fourteen years and caused the death of her husband, King Dasharatha. Termed *Lobha* in Sanskrit, greed is considered dangerous because it can take control of our minds. As illustrated through a few examples in this section, people engulfed by greed may not hesitate to engage in dastardly acts such as stealing, defrauding, attacking, and even killing others to acquire and possess their objects of greed.

1.5   When Greed Becomes Good

The Evolutionary Viewpoint

From an evolutionary perspective, there is an adaptive aspect of greed (Chen, 2018; Krekels & Pandelaere, 2015; Wang & Murnighan, 2011), where greed helped us survive in resource-scarce environments by motivating us to acquire more. Religions may denounce greed as a sin, but how do people renounce it when it is part of their evolutionary makeup? If greed is built into our neuropsychological system, can we escape it? Or rather, do we even want to escape it, especially if it continues to provide us with certain evolutionary advantages?

Although there are not many empirical studies that have investigated the evolutionary links of greed, literature is gradually building in the area. Kidd et al. (2013) provided indirect support for the evolutionary theory of greed when they found that children placed in an *unreliable* condition—where future access to resources was unpredictable were more likely to choose instant gratification compared to a *reliable* condition where the access was predictable. Similarly, Chen (2018) found that childhood environmental unpredictability was positively associated with greed.

We cannot (and should not) make literal inferences of the findings of these studies. If scarce and unpredictable environments tend to be associated with greedy choices, then is it possible that the scanty environment of Kenneth Lay's childhood deepened the greed within him? Possibly, but if that is the case, wasn't Lay as much as a victim as he was a perpetrator? If scarcity and uncertainty in childhood can make people greedier, would it be fair to create regulations that limit people from such backgrounds into positions of authority? Most people would agree that such policies should never happen, except perhaps within the bounds of a fictional novel or movie depicting some dystopian future.

In a famous scene from the Hollywood movie "Wall Street," the character of Gordon Gekko, a Wall Street maverick portrayed by Michael Douglas asserted, "I am not a destroyer of companies. I am a liberator of them! ... Greed, for lack of a better word, is good. Greed is right. Greed works. Greed clarifies, cuts through, and captures the essence of the evolutionary spirit. Greed, in all of its forms—greed for life, for money, for love, knowledge—has marked the upward surge of mankind" (Stone & Weiser, 1987, http://www.dailyscript.com/scripts/wall_street. html).

Gordon Gekko's character was roughly inspired by the life of Ivan Boesky, who like Kenneth Lay gained notoriety for his involvement in a major financial scam, in the 1980s. Gekko's speech in the movie was also inspired by a speech that Boesky had given in real life. The celebrated businessman that Boesky was, he had been invited to give the commencement address to business students of the University of California, Berkeley. At this even, Boesky proclaimed to a rapturous audience, "Greed is all right... Greed is healthy. You can be greedy and still feel good about yourself" (Shapiro, 2021, p. 96).

Similar to the story of Kenneth Lay, everyone lionized Boesky and wanted to emulate him before he was caught in the scam. However, unlike Lay, Boesky grew up in an affluent family that owned several delicatessens and taverns in Detroit, Michigan (Green, 2013).

The evolutionary explanation of greed is not that greed develops only when the environment is unpredictable but that greed may have provided certain survival advantages in those situations, which ultimately led to it becoming part of our psycho-physiological makeup. Greed is perhaps not distributed equally across all strata of society. However, history is replete with examples of people of all backgrounds displaying rapacious greed.

The Economic Viewpoint

If we give credence to the scientific discipline of evolutionary psychology, there is little doubt about how the acquisitive nature of greed must have played a significant role in our self-preservation and survival. Greed, in other words, is natural. However, natural should not automatically be deduced to be ethical or desirable. Doing so would be a naturalistic fallacy (Frankena, 1939), which the promoters of greed tend to engage in.

Greed may be taboo in most religions, but it is often celebrated in the world of business and economics. Adam Smith, who is often called the father of Economics and Capitalism, introduced the concept of self-interest and described it as the true engine of economic growth. In the classic *The Wealth of Nations*, he contended, "It is not from the benevolence of the butcher, the brewer, or the baker, that we expect our dinner, but from their regard to their own interest" (A. Smith, 1776/1937, p. 14).

Are Smith's words a direct validation of greed? Not exactly. In the Introduction to the 1937 edition of *The Wealth of Nations*, Max Lerner stated that Smith's "doctrine has been twisted in ways he would not have approved" (p. x) but he also acknowledged how "Smith was, to be sure, an unconscious mercenary in the service of a rising capitalist class in Europe. It is true that he gave a new dignity to greed and a new sanctification to the predatory impulses" (p. ix).

In defense of Smith, some scholars (e.g., Werhane, 1994; Wight, 2005) have argued that self-interest is not the same as greed. According to them, greed is the excessive pursuit of self-interest. The problem with this premise is that "excessive" is a subjective term that can be interpreted differently by different people. Both conceptually and empirically, it is extremely difficult to demarcate where self-interest ends and where greed begins (Wang & Murnighan, 2011; Wang et al., 2011). Greed and self-interest could also be merely a difference in who is making the appraisal. We are likely to consider our own acquisitive actions in terms of self-interest but judge the same in others as sinful greed. In other words, self-interest and greed may simply be verbal analogs of the same phenomenon that we use differently in consonance with our self-serving biases.

If Adam Smith helped provide legitimacy to greed in the world of business, Milton Friedman took it on steroids. Friedman, who in 1976 was awarded the Nobel Memorial Prize in Economic Sciences, is famously quoted for having said, "The social responsibility of business is to increase its profits" (Friedman, 1970, 2007). However, unlike what many of his critics believe, Friedman never explicitly said this to legitimize corporate misconduct, because in the same article he also stated that a business could focus on increasing their profits "so long as it stays within the rules of the game, which is to say, engages in open and free competition without deception or fraud." Whether or not Friedman encouraged greed in businesses may be open for some debate, but businessmen have certainly used his "statements to justify and legitimize their acts of questionable corporate excess" (Wang et al., 2011, p. 655).

Do all economists believe in the premise of "greed is good"? Certainly not. However, there is a substantial amount of empirical evidence showing a strong connection between the study of economics and self-centered behavior. Economics students and business students—who also take many economics courses—tend to engage in more self-interested behaviors and less other-oriented cooperative behaviors than their counterparts in other educational streams (B. Frank & Schulze, 2000; R. H. Frank et al., 1993; Marwell & Ames, 1981). In a study that compared academic dishonesty across various disciplines, McCabe et al. (2006) also found that business students cheat more than their nonbusiness-student peers.

There can certainly be alternative explanations for these findings. For example, students of a greedy disposition may be self-selecting into business and economics disciplines, or that there is possibly more competition in business and economics which puts greater pressure on them to cheat. To address some of these objections, a few studies have experimentally manipulated study participants' exposure to economics and still found that these exposures contributed to more favorable attitudes towards greed and self-interest maximizing behaviors among the participants (Wang et al., 2011).

Is it possible then that the subject of economics, which Kenneth Lay was so passionate about, also contributed to the development of avaricious greed within him?

1.6   CALL FOR ETHICS

Whatever we call it, greed or self-interest, capitalism relies on this force to function. As long as this force works for the benefit of all stakeholders, people would likely have no reasons to complain. However, we see again and again throughout the history of modern business that this force often pierces into the interests of many stakeholders, but especially those with less power (e.g., employees, local community, environment, etc.), and this is where the conflict begins.

In 2015, the German automaker Volkswagen was caught in an emissions scandal by the United States Environmental Protection Agency. The government expected all automakers to meet certain emission standards it set for all newly manufactured cars. Since meeting these standards translated to an increase in costs for the company, Volkswagen decided to take a shortcut. It simply installed a software program in its cars that would tighten the cars' emission-control systems temporarily when it detected that the car was being put through an emissions testing, thereby helping it pass the test. But once the car was off the test, it would go back to spewing toxic gases such as nitrogen oxides into the atmosphere at rates up to 40 times higher than the permissible limit (Schiermeier, 2015).

When Volkswagen's deception was caught, its CEO denied any wrongdoing until he could not anymore and had to resign from his position. Volkswagen's share prices dropped by 40% within 2 weeks. The company's future looked bleak. However, defying all expectations, the company slowly revived and even experienced a huge surge in sales in the years immediately after the post-scandal period. So what explained this revival? There were a combination of factors but a prominent one that deflected the attention from Volkswagen was that other major German and American car manufacturers had also practiced similar deception, which if they were found guilty would lead to fines amounting to $54 billion in Germany and criminal charges in the USA (Jung & Sharon, 2019). So, it was under everyone's "self-interest" to not create too much noise around the issue and let the issue pass.

This is not an isolated case. There are innumerable large organizations that easily get away with their wrongdoings. Coke and Pepsi continue to sell sugary drinks under the garb that there is "no compelling evidence" about their addictive nature and impact on childhood and adult obesity (Nestle, 2015). Smartphone and social media companies have deliberately installed specific features on their platforms that elicit compulsive and addictive responses in their users making them use them for prolonged periods of time (Hou et al., 2019; Hristova et al., 2020; Thorpe & Roper, 2019). The list goes on and on.

We do not wish to disparage the profit-making orientation of companies because this orientation does help people and companies succeed in a competitive marketplace. The only problem is that the unrestrained pursuit of self-interest usually comes at a huge cost to the environment, people, and society. It has led to the exploitation of natural resources and human beings. Forests are simply seen as sources of timber or as pieces of land that could be grabbed for some form of "land development" to garner profits. Human beings are seen as "resources" whose talents could be exploited for gains. Young women get commodified as sex objects to enhance sales. Children become ideal targets of advertisements because of the influence they have on the adult members of families. Everyone and everything is viewed with an instrumental lens. And perhaps the greatest irony is that even the act of giving (or charity) is decided based on the potential returns that the contribution could yield in terms of enhanced reputation and market value (Carroll & Shabana, 2010; Du et al., 2010). Is it any wonder that Kenneth Lay, Jeffrey Skilling, Bernie Madoff, and perhaps, all of the big fraudsters of recent times were also huge on philanthropy?

This is a lopsided approach to doing business, which is inherently unsustainable because there is no limit to our appetite for profits. To counter this trend, scholars and researchers have emphasized the importance of incorporating ethics into business. And sure, there has been a lot of talk about business ethics, especially over the last couple of decades (Floyd et al., 2013; Ghoshal, 2005; McCabe et al., 2006).

1.7   The Two Most Common Responses

All business organizations espouse to be conducting their businesses ethically. But how much of this is a real commitment to ethical principles, and how much of is empty talk designed to project an image of being ethical? Let's briefly analyze the two most common approaches that businesses have adopted in response to the call for ethics.

Green Capitalism

Many scholars have argued that materialism is one of the root causes of resource depletion, pollution, environmental degradation, and climate change (Dresner, 2012; Dryzek, 2013; Porritt, 1984). The obsessive pursuit of materialistic goals causes tremendous harm to the environment. It is estimated that some of these damages may take several centuries to reverse even under the hypothetical scenario of we causing no additional damage in the intervening period.

One of the approaches adopted by business organizations to counter the damages to the environment is innovation. These innovations aren't just restricted to the realm of technology but also expand into the areas of accounting and marketing. Sometimes described as "green capitalism" or "eco-capitalism," this approach aims to use the strengths of the capitalistic system to benefit the environment (Prothero & Fitchett, 2000). This approach has led to the creation and marketing of many innovative ideas, such as the use of various green technologies (e.g., LED lights in place of the energy-hungry incandescent bulbs), green taxes (where a certain tax is levied upon businesses that harm the environment), green tax credits (where organizations get tax deductions for adopting renewable energy options), and green labeling (where different labels are put on product packages to certify their environment-friendliness).

Green capitalism involves the adoption of business models where there can be economic advantages for adopting business practices that help sustain the environment, and it certainly has many merits. It is a pro-innovation approach that believes in the creative capacity of human beings to solve the world's problems. It may help the environment to a certain extent, but there is little evidence of it being sufficient enough to reverse the damage we are causing to the environment. For example, replacing gas-guzzling cars with low gas mileage cars, hybrid cars or electric cars may reduce the environmental impact of new cars, but there is also evidence of plug-in hybrids and electric cars increasing carbon dioxide emissions when they are used in regions where electricity is powered by coal. Further, if companies continue to produce and promote the purchase of more cars, whatever the type, how are we going to stop the overexploitation of the planet? It is for such reasons that there is growing skepticism about green capitalism (Bradshaw & Zwick, 2016; Dolan, 2002; R. Smith and World Economics Association, 2016).

Corporate Social Responsibility

Corporate Social Responsibility or CSR is an approach where companies voluntarily integrate the social and environmental concerns of people into their business operations (Dahlsrud, 2008). It can also be broadly classified as a form of green capitalism, as it is essentially a tool "strategically" used by organizations to meet the expectations of the society in a way that enhances its competitive success (Galbreath, 2009; Yuan et al., 2020).

CSR is one of the most researched topics in business. This research shows the strong positive impact that CSR initiatives can have on business organizations. But does CSR benefit the society and environment in as big a way as it does the firm? Lyon and Maxwell (2008) write that the welfare effects of CSR are difficult to establish and likely small.

Further, CSR has been used extensively by firms to project a positive image about themselves—called "greenwashing" (Cherry & Sneirson, 2010; de Freitas Netto et al., 2020; Mahoney et al., 2013). Studies have also found that companies sometimes use CSR to repair their reputation after a serious accounting restatement (Chakravarthy et al., 2014). A recent study even found that "firms that participate in illegal price fixing schemes increase their CSR initiatives around the time when they become the target of an antitrust investigation - not before" (Ferrés & Marcet, 2020). Overall, it can be said that the moral self-regulation of CSR has not been sufficient to overcome the negative effects of avaricious capitalism.

1.8   A Dharmic Alternative

As discussed in our brief overview, greed is clearly a problem in the capitalistic world that we live in. The narrative of self-interest maximization that has been the dominant paradigm within the economics and business literature has perhaps helped "legitimize and possibly even glorify greed" (Wang et al., 2011, p. 655). The net result has been that measures instituted to combat greed and/or minimize the damages caused by it—such as CSR, green innovations, and green bonds—have ironically become effective instruments to further greed.

So, what is the way forward? In this book, we argue that the practice of management—in the ever-changing contextual and interdependent environment that we live in—requires a holistic approach that recognizes businesses' need for profits while simultaneously nudging them in the direction of social and environmental responsibility. Specifically, we discuss a set of principles that is rooted in the Hindu philosophy and praxis of the Hindu Dhārmic tradition.

The tradition emphasizes the importance of adhering to dharma to minimize suffering and facilitate flourishing in our lives. Dharma is a Sanskrit word that shows up even in the oldest of Hindu literature, i.e., the Vedas. It is a complex word with many nuances in its meaning. We will touch upon these meanings in the forthcoming chapters, but for now, we provide a general interpretation of the term. For the purposes of this book, dharma can be understood as a set of ethical principles that aim to promote advancement and prosperity. It is held that the violation of these principles curtails our growth and often leads to unnecessary suffering. The story of Vasistha's Curse that we started this chapter also comes from this tradition. It is taken from an ancient Hindu text called the Nārada Purana. In the book, sage Nārada narrates this story to another sage (Maharshi Shaunaka) in response to the question, "Do good deeds cancel out bad deeds, or do people have to experience the consequences of both?" Currently, businesses operate under the premise that their good deeds cancel out any harm they bring to people and the environment. But is that how the world operates?

In the story, Prabhās had done innumerable great deeds throughout his life as a devatā (god), but he had to suffer the consequence of entertaining the thought of stealing. He didn't get a free pass, just because he was a god. Instead, he suffered consequences that were much more severe than what a human being would have suffered for a similar infraction. When Prabhās was reborn as a human being, he never got to enjoy the pleasures of marital life because his original infraction was partly caused by his infatuation with his wife. The Mahābhārata describes that Bhishma had a privileged birth and he also developed himself into one of the most capable, powerful, and ethical human beings that ever walked the face of Earth. Yet, life circumstances stole away most pleasures from his life. He even had to endure the pain of lying for 58 days on a bed of arrows that had pierced his entire body.

In the words of Maharshi Nārada,

Avashyam Eva Bhoktavyam Krutakarma Shubha Ashubam |
Naa Bhuktam Kshiyate Karma Kalpa-Koti-Shaitairapi ||

Translation: People will definitely experience the consequences of their kruta karma (actions). The karmas won't die out even after 10 million kalpas (1 kalpa = 4.32 billion years) till they have been given the appropriate consequences.

We may or may not agree with Nārada's assertion that we will inevitably enjoy or suffer the consequences of our actions. However, we do know that people tend to engage in more harmful behaviors when they believe that they can personally evade the consequences of their actions (Burrus et al., 2007; DeShay et al., 2021; Sanchirico, 2006). People use innumerable strategies to avoid negative consequences of their actions, from lying to sophisticated use of technology to cover their tracks. If something tangible is not feasible, then they may even pray to their beloved God for mercy and forgiveness. The Dhārmic tradition tries to outflank our psychological weaknesses by building a society around the value that both good and bad actions get their consequences; they do not cancel each other out.

1.9   Conclusion

The construction of any physical structure starts with laying a solid foundation regardless of the height or the spread of the structure. Be it a bridge or a building, the foundation bears most of its load. A strong foundation can save a structure from crumbling and eventually collapsing. It is perhaps for this reason that it is often said in Civil Engineering circles that a structure is as strong as its foundation. This is as much true for human beings and organizations as it is for buildings. Dharma is not foolproof, but it attempts to build a solid foundation so that human beings, organizations, communities, and nations can flourish and sustain for long periods of time. In the next chapter, we discuss some of the foundational principles of dharma and their relevance to the world of business.

References

Agarwal, S., Amromin, G., Ben-David, I., Chomsisengphet, S., & Evanoff, D. D. (2014). Predatory lending and the subprime crisis. *Journal of Financial Economics, 113*(1), 29–52.

Arnold, B., & De Lange, P. (2004). Enron: An examination of agency problems. *Critical Perspectives on Accounting, 15*(6–7), 751–765.

Baker, C. R. (2003). Investigating Enron as a public private partnership. *Accounting, Auditing & Accountability Journal*.

Benston, G. J. (2006). Fair-value accounting: A cautionary tale from Enron. *Journal of Accounting and Public Policy, 25*(4), 465–484.

Benston, G. J., & Hartgraves, A. L. (2002). Enron: What happened and what we can learn from it. *Journal of Accounting and Public Policy, 21*(2), 105–127.

Bloch, A. P. (1984). *A book of Jewish ethical concepts: Biblical and postbiblical.* KTAV Publishing House Inc.

Bradshaw, A., & Zwick, D. (2016). The field of business sustainability and the death drive: A radical intervention. *Journal of Business Ethics, 136*(2), 267–279.

Bratton, W. W. (2003). Enron, Sarbanes-Oxley and accounting: Rules versus principles versus rents. *Villanova Law Review, 48*, 1023.

Brown, R. E. (2005). Enron/Andersen: Crisis in US accounting and lessons for government. *Public Budgeting & Finance, 25*(3), 20–32.

Burrus, R. T., McGoldrick, K., & Schuhmann, P. W. (2007). Self-reports of student cheating: Does a definition of cheating matter? *The Journal of Economic Education, 38*(1), 3–16.

Carnegie, G. D., & Napier, C. J. (2010). Traditional accountants and business professionals: Portraying the accounting profession after Enron. *Accounting, Organizations and Society, 35*(3), 360–376.

Carroll, A. B., & Shabana, K. M. (2010). The business case for corporate social responsibility: A review of concepts, research and practice. *International Journal of Management Reviews, 12*(1), 85–105.

Chakravarthy, J., DeHaan, E., & Rajgopal, S. (2014). Reputation repair after a serious restatement. *The Accounting Review, 89*(4), 1329–1363.

Chen, B.-B. (2018). An evolutionary life history approach to understanding greed. *Personality and Individual Differences, 127*, 74–78.

Cherry, M. A., & Sneirson, J. F. (2010). Beyond profit: Rethinking corporate social responsibility and greenwashing after the BP oil disaster. *Tulane Law Review, 85*, 983.

Clark, W. W., & Demirag, I. (2002). Enron: The failure of corporate governance. *Journal of Corporate Citizenship*(8), 105–122.

Clarke, T. (2005). Accounting for Enron: Shareholder value and stakeholder interests. *Corporate Governance: An International Review, 13*(5), 598–612.

Dahlsrud, A. (2008). How corporate social responsibility is defined: An analysis of 37 definitions. *Corporate Social Responsibility and Environmental Management, 15*(1), 1–13.

David, J., Visvalingam, S., & Norberg, M. M. (2021). Why did all the toilet paper disappear? Distinguishing between panic buying and hoarding during COVID-19. *Psychiatry Research, 303*,. https://doi.org/10.1016/j.psychres.2021.114062

Davies, D. (2021). *Lying for money: How legendary frauds reveal the workings of the world*: Simon and Schuster.

de Freitas Netto, S. V., Sobral, M. F. F., Ribeiro, A. R. B., & da Luz Soares, G. R. (2020). Concepts and forms of greenwashing: A systematic review. *Environmental Sciences Europe, 32*(1), 1–12.

DeShay, R. A., Vasquez, A. G., & Vieraitis, L. M. (2021). "You Gotta Have a Plan so You Won't Get Caught": Managing the Risks of Street Tagging. *Deviant Behavior, 42*(9), 1112–1129.

Dillon, P., & Cannon, C. (2010). *Circle of Greed: The spectacular rise and fall of the lawyer who brought corporate America to its knees*. Crown.

Dolan, P. (2002). The sustainability of "sustainable consumption." *Journal of Macromarketing, 22*(2), 170–181.

Dresner, S. (2012). *The principles of sustainability*. Routledge.

Dryzek, J. S. (2013). *The politics of the earth: Environmental discourses*. Oxford university press.

Du, S., Bhattacharya, C. B., & Sen, S. (2010). Maximizing business returns to corporate social responsibility (CSR): The role of CSR communication. *International Journal of Management Reviews, 12*(1), 8–19.

Eckhaus, E., & Sheaffer, Z. (2018). Managerial hubris detection: The case of Enron. *Risk Management, 20*(4), 304–325.

Ferrés, D., & Marcet, F. (2020). Corporate social responsibility and corporate misconduct. *Journal of Banking and Finance*. https://doi.org/10.2139/ssrn.3620443

Floyd, L. A., Xu, F., Atkins, R., & Caldwell, C. (2013). Ethical outcomes and business ethics: Toward improving business ethics education. *Journal of Business Ethics, 117*(4), 753–776.

Frank, B., & Schulze, G. G. (2000). Does economics make citizens corrupt? *Journal of Economic Behavior & Organization, 43*(1), 101–113.

Frank, R. H., Gilovich, T., & Regan, D. T. (1993). Does studying economics inhibit cooperation? *Journal of Economic Perspectives, 7*(2), 159–171.

Frankena, W. K. (1939). The naturalistic fallacy. *Mind, 48*(192), 464–477.

Friedman, M. (1970). The social responsibility of business is to increase its profits. *New York Times Magazine, 13*, 32–33.

Friedman, M. (2007). The social responsibility of business is to increase its profits. In *Corporate ethics and corporate governance* (pp. 173–178): Springer.

Galbreath, J. (2009). Building corporate social responsibility into strategy. *European Business Review*.

Gambhirananda, S. (1984). *Bhagavad Gita: With the commentary of Shankaracharya: Advaita Ashrama*. A publication branch of Ramakrishna Math.

Gates, D. (2002, July 28). Greed R.I.P (for now). *Newsweek*. https://www.newsweek.com/greed-ripnow-147377.

Ghoshal, S. (2005). Bad management theories are destroying good management practices. *Academy of Management Learning & Education, 4*(1), 75–91.

Gini, A. (2004). Business, ethics, and leadership in a post Enron era. *Journal of Leadership & Organizational Studies, 11*(1), 9–15.

Goldberg, M. H. (1994). *The complete book of greed: The strange and amazing history of human excess*: William Morrow & Company.

Green, D. B. (2013, November 14). This day in Jewish history | 1986: A masterful wall street con man is arrested. *Haaretz*. https://www.haaretz.com/jewish/.premium-1986-wall-street-conman-arrested-1.5290528.

Hains, T. (2020). *Man Who Hoarded 18,000 Bottles Of Hand Sanitizer To Resell: I'm Not Sorry*. https://www.realclearpolitics.com/video/2020/03/15/man_who_hoarded_18000_bottles_of_hand_sanitizer_to_resell_im_not_sorry.html.

Hallman, C. (2019). *The 20 biggest bankruptcies in United States history*. https://www.titlemax.com/discovery-center/money-finance/20-biggest-bankruptcies-in-us-history/. Accessed October 17 2021.

Heath, J., & Norman, W. (2004). Stakeholder theory, corporate governance and public management: What can the history of state-run enterprises teach us in the post-Enron era? *Journal of Business Ethics, 53*(3), 247–265.

Hou, Y., Xiong, D., Jiang, T., Song, L., & Wang, Q. (2019). Social media addiction: Its impact, mediation, and intervention. *Cyberpsychology: Journal of psychosocial research on cyberspace, 13*(1).

Hristova, D., Jovicic, S., Göbl, B., & Slunecko, T. (2020). The social media game?: How gamification shapes our social media engagement. In *The Digital Gaming Handbook* (pp. 63–94): CRC Press.

http://blackfridaydeathcount.com/. Black Friday Death Count.

Johnson, C. E. (2003). *Enron's ethical collapse: Lessons for leadership educators*.

Jung, J. C., & Sharon, E. (2019). The Volkswagen emissions scandal and its aftermath. *Global Business and Organizational Excellence, 38*(4), 6–15.

Kaplan, M. (2020). *Black Friday's most gruesome injuries and deaths through the years*. https://nypost.com/article/black-fridays-most-gruesome-injuries-and-deaths-through-the-years/.

Kidd, C., Palmeri, H., & Aslin, R. N. (2013). Rational snacking: Young children's decision-making on the marshmallow task is moderated by beliefs about environmental reliability. *Cognition, 126*(1), 109–114.

Knottnerus, J. D., Ulsperger, J. S., Cummins, S., & Osteen, E. (2006). Exposing Enron: Media representations of ritualized deviance in corporate culture. *Crime, Media, Culture, 2*(2), 177–195.

Krekels, G., & Pandelaere, M. (2015). Dispositional greed. *Personality and Individual Differences, 74*, 225–230.

Kulik, B. W. (2005). Agency theory, reasoning and culture at Enron: In search of a solution. *Journal of Business Ethics, 59*(4), 347–360.

Lo, A. W., Repin, D. V., & Steenbarger, B. N. (2005). Fear and greed in financial markets: A clinical study of day-traders. *American Economic Review, 95*(2), 352–359.

Lyon, T. P., & Maxwell, J. W. (2008). Corporate social responsibility and the environment: A theoretical perspective. *Review of Environmental Economics and Policy, 2*(2), 240–260.

Mahoney, L. S., Thorne, L., Cecil, L., & LaGore, W. (2013). A research note on standalone corporate social responsibility reports: Signaling or greenwashing? *Critical Perspectives on Accounting, 24*(4–5), 350–359.

Markham, J. W. (2015). *A financial history of modern US corporate scandals: From Enron to reform.* Routledge.

Marwell, G., & Ames, R. E. (1981). Economists free ride, does anyone else?: Experiments on the provision of public goods. *Iournal of Public Economics, 15*(3), 295–310.

McCabe, D. L., Butterfield, K. D., & Trevino, L. K. (2006). Academic dishonesty in graduate business programs: Prevalence, causes, and proposed action. *Academy of Management Learning & Education, 5*(3), 294–305.

McLean, B., & Elkind, P. (2013). *The smartest guys in the room: The amazing rise and scandalous fall of Enron.* Penguin.

Nestle, M. (2015). *Soda politics: Taking on big soda (and winning).* Oxford University Press.

Oka, R., & Kuijt, I. (2014). Greed is bad, neutral, and good: A historical perspective on excessive accumulation and consumption. *Economic Anthropology, 1*(1), 30–48.

Ooghe, H., & De Prijcker, S. (2008). Failure processes and causes of company bankruptcy: A typology. *Management decision.*

Partnoy, F. (2010). *Infectious Greed: How deceit and risk corrupted the Financial Markets.* Profile Books.

Porritt, J. (1984). *Seeing green: The politics of ecology explained.* B. Blackwell.

Prothero, A., & Fitchett, J. A. (2000). Greening capitalism: Opportunities for a green commodity. *Journal of Macromarketing, 20*(1), 46–55.

Ronen, J. (2014). Post-enron reform: financial statement insurance, and GAAP re-visited. In *Accounting and regulation* (pp. 31–58). Springer.

Sanchirico, C. W. (2006). Detection avoidance. *New York University Law Review, 81*, 1331.

Schiermeier, Q. (2015). The science behind the Volkswagen emissions scandal. *Nature.* https://doi.org/10.1038/nature.2015.18426

Schwarcz, S. L. (2004). Rethinking the disclosure paradigm in a world of complexity. *University of Illinois Law Review,* 1.

Seeger, M. W., & Ulmer, R. R. (2003). Explaining Enron: Communication and responsible leadership. *Management Communication Quarterly, 17*(1), 58–84.

Shapiro, F. R. (Ed.). (2021). *The New Yale Book of Quotations*. Yale University Press.

Smith, A. (1776/1937). *An inquiry into the nature and causes of the wealth of nations*. Random House.

Smith, R., & World Economics Association (2016). *Green capitalism: the god that failed*. College Publications.

Stone, O., & Weiser, S. (1987). *Wall Street*. 20th Century Fox.

Swartz, M., & Watkins, S. (2004). *Power failure: The inside story of the collapse of Enron*. Broadway Business.

Takacs Haynes, K., Campbell, J. T., & Hitt, M. A. (2017). When more is not enough: Executive greed and its influence on shareholder wealth. *Journal of Management, 43*(2), 555–584.

This Day in Jewish History | 1986: A Masterful Wall Street Con Man Is Arrested. (2013, November 14). *Haaretz*.

Thorpe, A. S., & Roper, S. (2019). The ethics of gamification in a marketing context. *Journal of Business Ethics, 155*(2), 597–609.

Tickle, P. A. (2004). *Greed: The seven deadly sins*. Oxford University Press.

Toffler, B. L., & Reingold, J. (2004). *Final accounting: Ambition, greed, and the fall of Arthur Andersen*. Currency.

Venkatesananda, S. (1988). *Concise Ramayana of Valmiki*. SUNY Press.

Vinten, G. (2002). The corporate governance lessons of Enron. *Corporate Governance: The international journal of business in society*.

Wang, L., Malhotra, D., & Murnighan, J. K. (2011). Economics education and greed. *Academy of Management Learning & Education, 10*(4), 643–660.

Wang, L., & Murnighan, J. K. (2011). On greed. *Academy of Management Annals, 5*(1), 279–316.

Werhane, P. H. (1994). Adam Smith and his legacy for modern capitalism. *The Review of Metaphysics, 47*(3), 644–646.

Wheelwright, T. (2018). These states are at high risk for Black Friday violence. https://www.reviews.org/trends/high-risk-states-for-black-friday-violence/.

Wight, J. B. (2005). Adam Smith and greed. *Journal of Private Enterprise, 21*(1), 46.

Williams, M. (2010). *Uncontrolled risk: Lessons of Lehman Brothers and how systemic risk can still bring down the world financial system*. McGraw Hill Professional.

Wong, P. T. (2002). Lessons from the Enron debacle: Corporate culture matters. *Effective Executive*.

Yuan, Y., Lu, L. Y., Tian, G., & Yu, Y. (2020). Business strategy and corporate social responsibility. *Journal of Business Ethics, 162*(2), 359–377.

CHAPTER 2

What Is Dharma?

2.1 THE HINDU GREAT FLOOD

In the *Matsya Purāṇa* and *Vishnu Purāṇa* (ancient texts within the *Vaishnav* tradition of Hinduism), there is a story about a sage-king named Satyavrat (the literal meaning of the name is somebody who is committed to truth). On a particular day when Satyavrat was performing his daily ablutions in the river, a small fish came between his two palms seeking protection from a large fish that was trying to eat it. Satyavrat gently picked up the fish making a cup with his palm and placed it in his sacred stoup. He took the fish home and placed it in a small bowl.

The next morning, he noticed that the fish had grown too large for the bowl. So, he moved the fish to a larger bowl. The following day, the fish had even outgrown the bigger bowl, so Satyavrat moved it into the small tank in his palace. However, the following morning he noticed that even the tank was not sufficient for this fast-growing fish. So, he moved the fish to a nearby pond. The outgrowing of the fish continued, and the king kept moving the fish to a larger waterbody until he noticed that even the river was being too small for the fish. Satyavrat then moved the fish into the ocean.

The fish thanked the king for protecting him and promised to return the favor sometime. The fish explained that soon there was going to be a massive flood that would submerge most of Earth. The fish said it would

© The Author(s), under exclusive license to Springer Nature
Switzerland AG 2022
P. Mishra and S. Kalagnanam, *Managing by Dharma*, Palgrave Studies
in Workplace Spirituality and Fulfillment,
https://doi.org/10.1007/978-3-030-90669-6_2

help the king then. Given how fast the fish had grown, the king realized this was no ordinary fish and perhaps had some divine abilities of prescience. But he didn't want to depend on some promised help. He came back to his kingdom and started building a large ship.

Sometime later, there was indeed a great deluge. And as predicted, it started engulfing most of the land areas on Earth. A lot of plants, animals, and human beings were getting killed in this flood. However, Satyavrat was prepared. He had already built a huge ship. He boarded as many people and animals as he could in it and started sailing.

However, the current of the flood was too strong. It seemed like his ship would not withstand the harsh conditions for long. With land nowhere in sight, he started losing hope. It was at this time that the fish which the king had saved reappeared. It instructed Satyavrat to tie a rope to attach it with the ship. The fish then tugged Satyavrat's ship through the troubled waters to the top regions of Mount Meru which had not been engulfed by the great deluge.

According to the ancient texts, this is how humanity was saved from the great deluge. The fish that saved so many lives, according to these texts, was the first avatar (or manifestation) of Vishnu (the supreme God within the *Vaishnav* tradition) on Earth. The king, for having played an important role in saving human beings from annihilation, came to be known as Manu (literally means 'the man').

2.2   UNIVERSALITY OF THE GREAT FLOOD STORY

The great flood story is not exclusive to the Hindu tradition. Most Westerners would be familiar with the Biblical version of the story where Noah built a large ship on God's command that helped save himself, his family, and a few representatives of land animals to repopulate the Earth. Noah's story is a reproduction of the Babylonian epic of Gilgamesh. And there are many other variations of the story from lands as far apart as China, Kenya, and Hawaii.

Because of how widespread the 'mythology' of the great flood is, many scientists believe that the story may not be a myth but a collective memory of an actual event. The explanations provided by these scientists range from rising water levels towards the end of the last Ice Age to tsunamis caused by moving tectonic plates or a crashed comet (Piccardi & Masse 2007; Ryan & Pitman, 2000); these events are estimated to have happened some six to seven thousand years ago.

One or more of these explanations could be plausible, but what is interesting is that the stories around this cataclysmic event, while being similar in some respects, are also dramatically different in important details. This is perhaps a reflection of the differing values across these cultures. And in the next section, we will analyze the Hindu version of the story to decode some key values within the dharmic tradition.

2.3 THE THREE PILLARS OF DHARMA

Why was king Satyavrat given the title of "the man"? His actions certainly saved him and many others from being killed in the great flood, but what are the bases of those actions? They clearly weren't impulsive actions that he took to face the immediate challenges in front of him. In this section, we discuss the values that king Satyavrat embodied, which ultimately made him deserving of the title, Manu. We think there are three values here, and they represent the core of what is dharma in the Hindu tradition (Fig. 2.1).

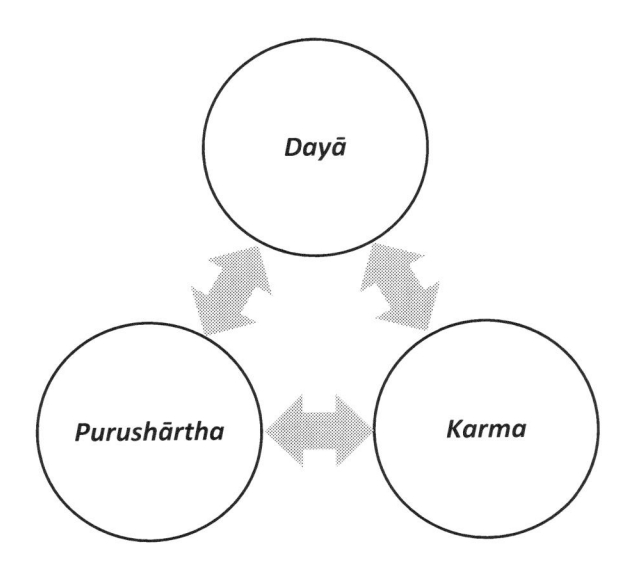

Fig. 2.1 The three pillars of Dharma

Dayā

The great flood story is not an exclusive feature of the Hindu tradition. However, the events that preceded the flood are unique to the Hindu version of the story. Specifically, the king saved a small fish in danger and went to extraordinary lengths nurturing it till it was big enough to take care of itself. This is referred to as *dayā* (or compassion) in Sanskrit. *Dayā* involves putting forth whatever effort is necessary to take care of the small and weak. According to the *Matsya Purāṇa*, *dayā* entails treating all living beings as if they are one's own self.

The word compassion in English literally means "to suffer together." This highlights the emotional component of the word. Most psychologists also tend to emphasize the feelings component of compassion in their definitions (Condon & Feldman Barrett, 2013; Goetz et al., 2010; Nussbaum, 1996). The Hindu tradition, although does not ignore this emotional dimension, provides greater emphasis on action. To be compassionate towards others, not just in thought but also in action is dharma.

Relating the concept of *dayā* to business ethics would mean that it is not enough for people and businesses to be emotionally sensitive to the suffering of others; one also has to take the necessary actions to alleviate the suffering. In the world today which is dominated by social media, we see people and companies publicly expressing sentiments of concern on different social and environmental issues. However, most of them do not do anything about those issues. And sometimes they are even caught practicing the opposite of what they preach.

What Dayā *Is Not?*

Compassion is the bedrock of dharma, but compassion hypocrisy is not. Unfortunately, compassion hypocrisy may be as common if not more common as real compassion. Here are a few recent examples pertaining to the hypocritical compassion shown for the environment. Murphy (2019) reported in the *National Post* that the founders of Google organized a 3-day summit with the rich and famous in Sicily to discuss the enormous negative impact of fossil fuels on the environment. But the biggest irony of the event was that 114 of the approximately 300 participants arrived at the summit in their gas-guzzling private jets (as per local flight records), and a significant number came in personal super-yachts that gobble up even more fossil fuel. Similarly, Fernyhough (2020) reported that the big four banks of Australia, while vociferously pledging their support to the 2015 Paris Climate Accords, had collectively invested over \$35.5 billion in the fossil fuel industry since 2016.

Compassion hypocrisy is not limited to corporations alone and happens widely at the individual level as well. A large percentage of the guests at the Google environmental summit after all were not representatives of corporations but of themselves and their own brands (e.g., Leonardo DiCaprio, Katy Perry, Nick Jonas, Priyanka Chopra, Woody Harrelson, Orlando Bloom, Sacha Baron Cohen, and many other celebrities). It is possible that many of these influencers do not even believe their own words. What else would explain Al Gore and Barrack Obama purchasing multi-million-dollar beachfront properties while talking in the most graphic terms about the seeming inevitability of melting ice caps and rising sea levels?

What we have identified as compassion hypocrisy is not just an observation based on isolated cases. Empirical research is starting to build upon this phenomenon. For example, recent studies on the habits of conservationists and climate change researchers show that they engage in many environmentally harmful behaviors, sometimes even more than their counterparts who are not working for the preservation of the environment (Balmford et al., 2017; Whitmarsh et al., 2020). Even scientists are not immune to this hypocrisy.

Empirical research is also building upon a phenomenon called moral grandstanding, where people and companies engage in a lot of moral talks by expressing their solidarity with different disadvantaged groups but all for self-promotion alone (Grubbs et al., 2019; Tosi & Warmke, 2016). Moral grandstanding (or virtue signaling, as it is called in the vernacular) has the appearance of *dayā* but it is not because of the predominant motivation being self-enhancement.

Purushārtha

The word, *purushārtha*, has three related meanings in the dharmic literature. One interpretation of the word is goal and not just any goal but a worthwhile goal. There are four broad categories of such goals in the dharmic tradition, and we will discuss them a little later in the chapter. The second meaning of the word is a focused effort that is directed towards the achievement of our goals. Finally, *purushārtha* also refers

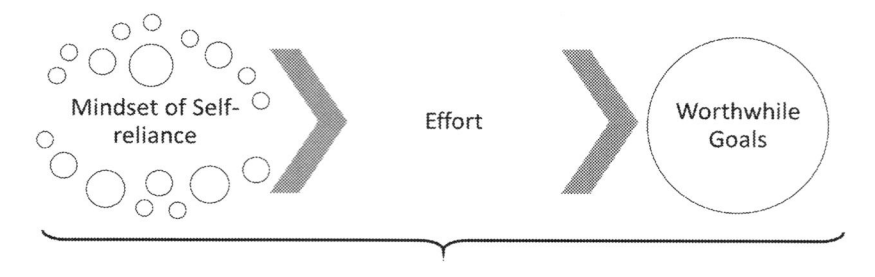

Purushārtha

Fig. 2.2 The Purushārtha philosophy

to the mindset where you rely on the power of your effort to realize whatever goals that you wish to achieve.

The philosophy of *purushārtha* essentially advocates that one should have worthwhile goals and rely on the power of one's own effort to realize them. In the great flood story, when Manu learns about the looming flood, he did not wish it away or rely on the promise of the fish to come to his rescue. Manu was an industrious person who relied on his effort to achieve his goals and to deal with probable challenges. So, he took matters into his own hands and built a massive ship in preparation for the incoming deluge. This is *purushārtha.*

In his bestseller, *12 Rules for Life: An Antidote to Chaos,* Jordan Peterson (2018) interprets Noah's story as being archetypal of how things can sometimes go completely wrong in our lives. He recommends that the way to deal with such chaotic events is to *work* on building one's strength so that one is ready to deal with life's challenges. Peterson's interpretation of Noah's story would be in agreement with the value of *purushārtha* (Fig. 2.2).

What Purushārtha *Is Not?*

Many people tend to have extremely romantic visions about morality. According to them, it is moral or dharmic, only when you are serving others, and ideally at some personal cost. The idea of *purushārtha* negates such impractical ideals of dharma. *Dayā,* the first dimension of dharma, certainly is other-oriented and encourages selfless concern and action for the well-being of others. But living one's life based on *dayā* alone is akin to walking on one leg when you have two.

The dimension of *purushārtha* makes it clear that there is nothing immoral (or *adhārmic*) about pursuing one's self-interest. In this sense, the idea of *purushārtha* is similar to the Western philosophy of ethical egoism, which says that moral agents ought to act in their self-interest. But there is also a key difference. Facione et al. (1978) defined ethical egoism as "the view that human conduct should be based *exclusively* on self-interest." Like ethical egoism, the *purushārtha* model also encourages people to pursue self-interest, and even with full vigor, but never exclusively. *Purushārtha* is not the *exclusive* pursuit of self-interest.

Karma

Manu's story also illustrates another key feature of the dharmic tradition, i.e., the concept of Karma, according to which, all actions have consequences. Manu performed good karma when he compassionately saved the fish and went several extra metaphorical miles taking care of it. Manu also performed good karma when he took hundred percent responsibility for the situation that he was in. He did not lament his fate that he would have to face a cataclysmic deluge that had the potential of destroying everything he valued. Instead, he got busy building a large ship that could potentially withstand the great deluge and save the lives of many beings. According to the law of karma, these good karmas were ultimately the reason that fate favored him in the form of support that he received from God.

What is the definition of *good* karma? We will answer this question in the next section of this chapter. But when it comes to the mechanism of how karma works, it is held that good karmas always lead to desirable consequences and bad karmas bring undesirable consequences. As explained in Chapter 1, the good and bad karmas do not cancel each other out. Rather, they each cause their own consequences. Also, as illustrated in Chapter 1's opening story, the consequences aren't always immediate and may fructify in a later birth.

Many people in the modern world do not believe in the idea of reincarnation. However, the idea of reincarnation is an integral part of all religions within the dharmic tradition (viz., Hinduism and its offshoots, Buddhism, Jainism, and Sikhism). All these religions hold the view that the true self of any living being is not its physical self. It is only the physical self that perishes after biological death, but the spiritual self (called *ātmā*)—that is considered the real self—journeys ahead. The journey ahead can take several paths, one of which is beginning a new life in a different living being.

In other words, the law of karma is completely intertwined with reincarnation. Without reincarnation, there can be no fair functioning of the law of karma. For example, imagine a situation in which a person in the last moments before his natural death unjustly shoots another human being and kills him. How can this killer get a fair cosmic retribution for his cruel action unless he gets it in another life? The concept of reincarnation helps logically resolve such anomalies (and many others, but we cannot discuss them here because they are beyond the scope of this book).

Be it reincarnation, karma, or even the concept of God(s)—singular and plural—all are scientifically unverifiable. But as long as people believe in one or more of these concepts, these beliefs will continue to impact their actions. In the context of business ethics, beliefs about karma can similarly influence how people act in their business dealings.

Although there isn't much empirical research focusing on the influence of karmic beliefs (White et al., 2019), there is plenty of research on a related construct called belief in a just world. According to Lerner (1980), human beings have a need to believe in justice, and the belief in a just world is the idea that people get what they deserve. The karmic belief system is an attractive proposition to people because it provides a psychological relief that the world is not an unjust place.

Both the belief in a just world and karma can justifiably be described as delusions of the mind (Lerner, 1980) because life is not fair. However, numerous studies have shown that belief in a just world is associated with enhanced happiness (Correia & Vala, 2004; Upenieks et al., 2021) and helping attitudes (Correia et al., 2016; Igou et al., 2021). Research also shows that the opposite worldview, specifically the belief in an unjust world, is associated with high levels of stress, anxiety, aggression, self-handicapping behaviors, and even criminal behaviors (Baron, 2003; Gau & Brunson, 2015; Lewis, 2016; Liang & Borders, 2012).

In a recently published study, Nudelman and Otto (2021) performed a meta-analysis of the existing literature on the connections between the belief in a just world and the personality trait of conscientiousness. They found that the belief in a just world was positively associated with an internal locus of control and some of the most desirable facets of conscientiousness, viz. self-efficacy, achievement striving, and self-discipline.

The above studies provide strong indirect evidence in favor of the Hindu karmic worldview. All businessmen strive for success. The belief in karma can be an invaluable mental resource because it enhances our faith in a just world and puts us in an optimistic state of mind that is critical to sustaining achievement motivation. Through its positive effects on altruistic attitudes, karmic beliefs also help mitigate the dangers of over-striving for success (that we detailed in Chapter 1).

What Karma *Is Not?*

The word karma is now part of the English vocabulary, but it is often mistakenly equated with fatalism. The truth is that there is no place for fatalism in dharma. The concept of *purushārtha*, which is one of the pillars of dharma, makes it explicit that we should not rely on fate and instead take the matter into our hands to change our destiny. As explained, *dayā* also is not just about feeling sorry for others but taking the necessary actions to alleviate others' suffering. Similarly, the concept of karma also holds that our actions (karma) alone determine our destinies.

Then, why do so many people mix up karma with fatalism? For example, Keith (1925) wrote, "The conception of *Karman* (a variation of the word, karma) serves indeed in an excellent way to defend and protect the established order of things, but it is essentially fatalistic; and fatalism is not for a normal mind a good incentive to moral progress." It might be the case that some people have deliberately misrepresented karma for their selfish ends. However, there can also be genuine confusion about karma. And this confusion probably arises from the fact that karmic consequences are causally opaque with no specific time limits on when and where they will manifest (Bronkhorst, 2011). For example, if I am suffering misfortunes in my present life because of some wrong deeds that I did in a past birth that I can't even remember, isn't karma fatalistic?

We think it will be easier to understand *karma* if we discuss it in conjunction with *purushārtha* and *dayā*. As already explained, *purushārtha* is about taking charge of one's own life. It is about the belief that I control my life. It is very explicitly the opposite of fatalism and a desirable quality to have. However, such beliefs of self-assurance and confidence can easily backfire when taken to the extreme. There is a large body of literature in the field of psychology that has examined the dark side of such confidence and optimism (Dillard et al., 2009; Kasser &

Ryan, 1993; Shepperd et al., 2015). It is beyond the scope of this book to delve deep into that literature, but suffice it to say that self-reliance, confidence, and optimism, when taken to a little too far often lead to many undesirable outcomes, such as depression, quitting, addictions, and lowered productivity. In her brilliant book, *Bright-sided: How Positive Thinking is Undermining America* Barbara Ehrenreich (2009) provides numerous real-life examples illustrating the negative impact that unrestrained positive beliefs of we controlling own destiny has on our health (physical, financial and social) and the economy. Similarly, *dayā* too can easily make people conceited. "I am this great generous person that saves the world!" There is a sizable body of literature that has explored such dark sides of altruism (Furnham et al., 2016; Oakley et al., 2011; Saito, 2015).

In simple words, the idea that we can and ought to take full control of our and others' lives is both unrealistic and undesirable. So, how do we put some restraints on the idea of *purushārtha* and *dayā* such that there are no spillovers into their dark sides? This is where the theory of karma comes into the picture. It provides a very realistic picture of life by acknowledging that there are several aspects of our life which we did not consciously earn in this life with our efforts.

The karma theory recognizes the fact that we have had little to no control over many aspects of our lives. For example, I had no control over where and to whom I was born, although these factors had a significant influence on my life. Even the opportunities (and setbacks) that I had in later life were not entirely my conscious creation but were sheer luck of being in the right (or wrong) place at the right (wrong) time. All these aspects of life that fell our way without we having done anything to earn them are explained as the karmic consequences of our actions in past births. The karmic explanations do not mean that we have had no control over our life (as has been mistakenly assumed by some); the explanations instead mean that we have had only partial control. The karmic explanations do not mean that we cannot influence our future; rather, they mean that we do have a significant influence over our future. The way our past actions (from present and past births) influenced our present circumstances, the same way our present actions will influence our future (in the present and future lives).

In simple words, karma neither is the belief of "I control everything," nor is it a fatalistic resignation over one's circumstances or victim-blaming of other people's circumstances. Karma is forward-oriented. It makes us realize that we can only control our present actions, but we do not have full control over the results that we aspire to attain. That's because future results will be influenced not just by our effort but also by numerous other factors that we have little to no control over. Some people call these uncontrolled factors luck. The karma theory just puts them under the category of *prārabdha karmas*, which are the effects of our actions from previous births that got carried forward to the current birth. The tradition holds that we cannot eliminate the effects of *prārabdha karmas*, but we can certainly mitigate or amplify those effects by choosing to act appropriately in the present. Through this process, it balances the negative aspects of self-reliance with humility, and the negative aspects of fatalistic belief in luck with the control that comes from focusing only on one's effort.

2.4   WHAT IS DHARMA?

In the West, the term Dharma is mostly associated with the teachings of the Buddha. The term Dharma that resonated so much with the Buddha, however, was already present in the Rig Veda, the oldest known Sanskrit text in the world. According to astronomical references found in the verses of the Rig Veda, it is considered to be from around 4,000 BCE, although the estimates vary from as early as 12,000 BCE to 1,500 BCE.

Is Dharma the Same as Religion?

In India, the word Dharma has become a colloquial Hindi translation for religion. Dharma, however, is not the same as religion. The meanings of words change over time, and people can certainly use a word any way they wish to as long as there is some concurrence in its meaning between sufficient numbers of people. However, if we examine the formal definitions of the words, we see that they differ significantly in their meanings.

Both the Webster and Oxford English dictionaries define religion as a system of faith and worship that is associated with belief in, obedience to, and reverence for a god or gods. In other words, the defining characteristic of religion is a belief in certain supernatural power. Dharma, in contrast, does not require any faith in god(s). Historically, there have been schools of thought within the dharmic tradition that expressly denied the existence of God (such as the Chārvāka school) or was ambiguous about it (such as the original ideas held by Buddha) (Chatterjee & Datta, 2016).

The word dharma, like many other Sanskrit words, does not have an exact translation in English. However, if we insist on a single-word translation of dharma, the closest in meaning will be ethics. Ethics typically refers to a set of moral principles that should govern people's behavior. Similar to ethics, dharma constitutes a set of principles that it recommends people to live by. However, these principles are less about morality where people tend to be judged based on certain arbitrary standards and more about wisdom. The idea behind the dharmic principles is that they help in the flourishing of individuals. Living according to dharmic principles means we are moving in the direction of fulfilling our full potential. Thus, it is considered wise to incorporate them into our lives. However, there isn't necessarily anything immoral or evil about not following dharma. Not following dharma only means not living in harmony with the world, which translates into a stunted life where we are unhappy and more stressed than is necessary.

The Etymology of Dharma

Dharma is a Sanskrit word that comes from the root *Dhri*, which means "to support, sustain, or hold together." *Dhri* is the root for many other Sanskrit words, such as *dhrit* (to hold or maintain), dhārayati (holds together), *dhāraṇa* (to sustain attention or to hold it firm), *Dhrūva* (North Star—the star that holds still), and *dhriti* (courage). Thus, according to the etymological origins of the word, dharma is that which upholds or that which sustains and brings stability. Within the Hindu tradition, dharma refers to a set of principles that nourishes, supports, and sustains the growth of the self, society, and the entire world. Dharma is that which supports or holds everyone and everything together (Mehta, 2011).

In the world of business today, sustainability is a buzzword. But based on the etymological roots, dharma would be the original word for sustainability. The words dharma and sustainability can be used interchangeably because the fundamental aim of dharma is to sustain. A dharmic approach to business is that which helps sustain it. Dharma is sustainable thinking, and *dharmāchāra* refers to all those practices that promote sustainability.

Maharshi Vyāsa's Definition

For many people, dharma seems to be an abstruse and complicated subject. However, according to the prominent ancient sages within the Hindu tradition, the essence of dharma is very simple. The legendary Maharshi Vyāsa, who is regarded as the compiler of all the Vedas and wrote the Mahabharata, said this about dharma:

Ashtādasha Purāṇām Sāram Vyāsena Kīrtitam |
Paropakārah Punyāya Pāpāya Parapīdanam ||

"The essence of the eighteen major *Purāṇa s* can easily be summed up as follows: Helping others is good and hurting others is bad."

According to Vyāsa, helping others and not hurting others are the two foundational principles of dharma. Vyāsa's *shlokā* also provides insights into the definition of good and bad. *Punya* or good karma is that which benefits people, and *pāpa* or bad karma is that which harms them. *Punya* and *pāpa* are sometimes incorrectly translated in English as virtue and sin. There is no concept of sin within Hinduism, at least not the way sin is defined in the Abrahamic religions. *Punya* is not an act that is necessarily rewarded by God. Similarly, *papa* is not an immoral act that would be punished by God. Instead, the dharmic tradition holds that the nature of *punya* and *pāpa* activities are such that they hold the seeds of future pleasure and pain, respectively.

We are being dharmic when we strive to make things better for the world; we are being dharmic when we do not engage in actions that can potentially harm others. In the real-life, it may not always be clear how our actions benefit or harm others. However, that cannot be an excuse for us to give up trying to figure out the consequences of our actions.

Let's take the case of the Hippocratic Oath for physicians, which famously says, "first, do no harm." The oath does not mean that physicians should never conduct any procedures that can potentially harm their patients. If that were the case, there would be no surgeries, X-rays, and innumerable other medical procedures in this world. Given the high variance that there exists in how different people respond to different treatments, it may be impossible for physicians to determine in advance if a particular procedure will be 100% safe for a patient. The idea of doing no harm then is not permission for inaction. Instead, it means that physicians should do everything in their capacity to remain aware of the potential risks, inform the patients about them (if possible), and do everything within their capacity to eliminate or minimize risks.

Vyāsa's summation of dharma might give the impression that dharma is all only about helping *others* (*Paropakāram*) and not hurting *others* (*Parapīdanam*). Does dharma ignore the needs of the self? Making such an interpretation would be incorrect. Vyāsa emphasizes other-orientation simply because biology already ensures that all living creatures instinctively act for their own and/or kin's survival. Caring for others, however, is not always automatic and requires an enhanced level of awareness and effort. However, the overall effect of such other-orientedness is a happy and sustainable society. Vyāsa emphasizes this with the following words in the Karna Parva of the Mahabharata (8.69.58):

dhāraṇāddharmamityāhurdharmo dhārayate prajāḥ |

"That which supports, that which holds together the people (of the universe), that is Dharma."

Maharshi Kanada's Definition

Maharshi Kanada the founder of the *Vaisheshika* philosophy—one of the six principal schools of Vedic Hindu philosophy—defined dharma with the following words:

Yato'bhyudaya-nihshreyasa siddhiḥ sa Dharmaḥ | (Kanada 1,1.2)

"That which sustainably enhances happiness and ceases suffering is dharma. The ultimate aim of dharma is to attain *nihshreyasa* (or eternal bliss)."

Like Vyāsa, sage Kanada also defines dharma in terms of enhancing benefits and reducing harm, but he does not say that the actions have to be oriented towards others to qualify as dharma. Instead, he says that we ought to aim to enhance happiness and reduce suffering in a lasting way.

Saint Madhvacharya, one of the chief proponents of the *Dvaita* school of philosophy, also said something very similar. In in his commentary on *Parāshāra Smriti*, said:

abhyudaya-niśreyase sādhanasattvena dhārayati iti dharmaḥ |

"Dharma refers to all those practices that promote progress and happiness (*abhyudaya*), and relieve suffering such that we can experience sustainable bliss (*niśreyasa*)."

The two keywords in Kanada's couplet are *Abhyudaya* and *Nihshreyasa*. *Abhyudaya* signifies rise, progress, and an increase in happiness and prosperity. *Nihshreyasa* literally means the total cessation of pain and suffering that translates into eternal happiness. These words emphasize the importance of our *āchāra* (or efforts) being directed towards making happiness sustainable. A lot of things can give us temporary happiness and even bliss, but most of these things do not give us lasting happiness. Some even cause more suffering in the long term. For example, injecting ourselves with some narcotic drug, such as heroin, cannot be dharmic because it causes enormous suffering in the long term even if it may give temporary states of blissfulness.

2.5 TRANSCENDING THE LAWS OF EVOLUTION

Truly, dharma is not as complicated a subject as we sometimes believe it to be. Maharshi Vyāsa's verse explains that dharma is about moving from self-interest to other-interest. He does not say that self-interest is *adhārmic* (or immoral), because basic survival would be impossible if there was no self-interest. However, his point is that lasting happiness that we all desire would be impossible as long as we are solely focused on self-interest.

While researching for this book, we stumbled on an article that made a similar point. In this article, Martin Jacques (2004), lamented the erosion of humanity by the selfish, market-driven society. The evidence of this erosion, he argued, lied in the lonely, unhappy, and isolated lives that people live today despite being surrounded by all kinds of material comforts. There is certainly a large body of evidence in support of the argument that stress, unhappiness, depression, and addictions have risen significantly in our societies (Sachs, 2019). Self-centered thinking is unlikely to give us the deep and sustainable experience of happiness that we all desire.

Matsyanyāya

The assertion that "a selfish, market-driven society is eroding our very humanity" might be considered by some to be too simplistic, but it certainly resonates with the wisdom coming from the Hindu dhārmic tradition. This tradition describes two broad types of laws: the law of the jungle (referred to as *matsyanyāya*) where "might is right," and the law of dharma that enables the flourishing of everyone in the society.

Matsyanyāya literally refers to the law of the fish world (*matsya* means fish and *nyāya* means law). It refers to a world where the bigger fish eats the smaller ones. It's a world where the mighty rule. *Matsyanyāya* is literally the law of the animal world. Several thousands of years ago, *matsyanyāya* was how even human beings lived. This was a world of the survival of the fittest. The physically stronger abused, enslaved, and exploited the weak for their selfish gains.

The world of *matsyanyāya* may be extremely unattractive to the weak. But what if I am very strong? Why should I bother about *matsyanyāya*? Won't I get the maximum spoils in such a world?

We do not have to believe in the great flood story of Manu. It could just be a mythological story. However, it would be unwise to discard the psychological truths that often remain embedded in mythological stories. It is a misconception that only the weak suffer in the world of *matsyanyāya*. For example, primatologist Frans de Waal (2007) has found in his decades of research on chimpanzees that even the strongest of the chimps often get violently taken down by coalitions of weaker opponents who are vying for the same position of power. The new power-holders enjoy their power for some time before they too get overthrown by new challengers. The cycle of violence and surrounding insecurity continues. In the world of *matsyanyāya*, it is not just the weak who suffer. Even the strong have to live in constant anxiety of being conquered and crushed by somebody stronger and meaner.

Metaphorically, human beings developed the potential to transition out of the *matsyanyāya* stage with Manu, the man, pioneering an alternative way of living, where human beings were not constantly battling each other for their survival. He proposed a set of laws that would not only alleviate the suffering of the weak but also provide security to the strong.

It was important that such a system was created that minimized suffering of all sections of the society. The laws of dharma not only accomplished that but also simultaneously provided a platform that ensured that everyone got the opportunity to progress and flourish. Thus, with the strong ruling over and eating the weak, *matsyanyāya*, continued in the natural world. However, with dharma, human beings started taking care of the weak (*dayā*). Instead of feeling helpless about the situations that they were in, they started relying on their effort to change their destinies (*purushārtha*). And they started respecting the cosmic rules of justice (*karma*). The strengthening of the three pillars of dharma essentially leads to the establishment of *Sanskriti* (or human civilization). Dharma, in other words, is elevating oneself above the evolutionary forces that control all living creatures.

From a biological perspective, human beings are animals too. They belong to the *Homo Sapiens* species. Humans and animals share an enormous amount of similarities at the anatomical and physiological levels. In other words, there is no denying that the evolutionary mechanisms extend into human beings as well. However, there are also dimensions on which we human beings differ significantly from animals. The critical and creative thinking abilities of human beings are infinitely higher than what has been observed in animals. Human beings also possess extraordinarily higher abilities to understand other people by ascribing mental states to them—called the theory of mind (Baron-Cohen et al., 1985; Gallagher & Frith, 2003). In the Yogic literature, human beings and animals are different on several inner faculties, which are *chitta* (advanced consciousness), *buddhi* (rational intellectual abilities), *manas* (complex emotions), and *ahankāra* (egoism). The differences in these abilities ultimately lead to us functioning at varying levels of awareness.

The Pancha *Koshas*

According to the *Taittiriya Upanishad* (Chinmayananda, 2014) and *Vivekachudamani* (Shankaracharya, 1981), the divine spirit (*ātmā*) is at the core of all living creatures and is regarded as the true self. However, few of us have an experiential awareness of this divine spirit, and that is because the *ātmā* is encompassed by five different levels of awareness, known as the *pancha koshas* (literally five layers) (Fig. 2.3).

The outermost and grossest level of awareness is that of the physical body (*Annamaya Kosha*). We are aware of our *Annamaya Kosha* when we are focused on our bodily needs such as food, water, sex, sleep, and safety. Both animals and human beings possess good awareness of the *Annamaya Kosha*. The next level of awareness is a little more subtle than the physical body and focuses on the breath and energy systems of the body

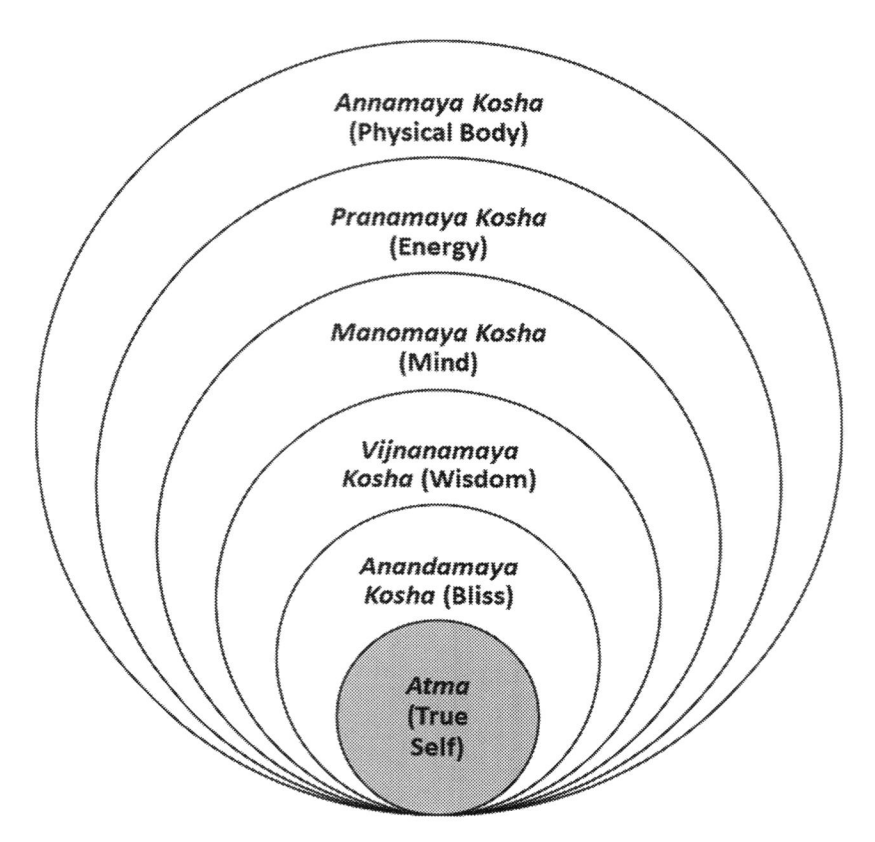

Fig. 2.3 The five levels of awareness

(*Prānamaya Kosha*). Both animals and human beings have awareness of this level, although, in our modern distracted world, the animals might be in greater tune with their energy systems than that of the majority of human beings. However, the next three levels of consciousness tend to be more dominant in human beings.

Manomaya Kosha refers to our psychological self that is preoccupied with innumerable thoughts and emotions. The neurological equate of the *manomaya kosha* would be the activity that is observed in the default-mode network of the brain, which consists of areas that are typically active during the times we are not actively engaged in any intellectual activity

(Raichle, 2015; Whitfield-Gabrieli & Ford, 2012). Most of the thoughts and emotions associated with tend to be self-referential in nature—for example, labeling oneself as lonely or fantasizing about a romantic vacation in Paris. The Yogic literature recommends people to not restrict their awareness to the *manomaya kosha*, and this is upheld by modern neurological research that has found that higher activity in the default-mode network is associated with greater anxiety, loneliness, and depression (Coutinho et al., 2016; Imperatori et al., 2019; Zhao et al., 2007).

Vijñānamaya Kosha is the next layer and is associated with higher psychological faculties such as logical thinking, creative thinking, and wisdom. A key feature of functioning in the *vijñānamaya kosha* is that one is not self-centered in one's thinking and is productively engaged in more abstract and creative thoughts. There is a large body of research in the field of psychology exploring the impact of such thinking, and they all point in the direction of us being happier when we function at this level (Bergsma & Ardelt, 2012; Ceci & Kumar, 2016; Csikszentmihalyi, 1997). This primarily happens because we tend to engage in less self-referential thinking when we are functioning at this level.

Lastly, the subtlest and deepest layer is the *Ānandamaya Kosha*, where there is a profound experiential awareness of our spiritual self or the *ātmā*. On an electroencephalogram, this may show up as sustained gamma waves, which are characterized by feelings of continuous bliss (Berkovich-Ohana, 2017; Kaufman, 2005; Stapleton et al., 2020; Vialatte et al., 2009). Only the advanced yogis and meditation practitioners succeed in keeping their awareness at the level of *Ānandamaya Kosha*, because it takes years of *sadhana* (disciplined spiritual practice) to reach the stage of surrendering one's ego and connect with the all-encompassing divine spirit. Most human beings tend to have only an intellectual awareness of the *ātmā*, which depending on the nature of those thoughts, would be functioning at the *Manomaya Kosha* or *Vijñānamaya Kosha* levels.

The point of our discussion of the *pancha koshas* is that human beings are much more than the self-interest-focused man conceptualized by the economists (Smith, 1776/1937; Miller, 2001; Friedman, 1962/2009, 1970). In an overly competitive world, one may not be able to eliminate self-interest-focused thinking. However, the more we succeed in expanding our thinking from the self to others, and maybe even to the common divinity that pervades all of us, we will be happier in our lives.

2.6   Conclusion

Some scholars, such as Fløistad (2014), assert that the problems of our times are a sign of the failure of the field of ethics. The "deep crisis" (Fløistad, 2014) that the discipline of ethics faces could be because of faulty premises within the dominant models of ethics. Or as suggested by Passmore (2004), it may have arisen because of the failure of the ethics philosophers "to make any contact with the general culture of the time," or both.

It is certainly true that some aspects of the challenges that we face today are unique to the times that we live in. However, we can also say with confidence that the fundamental nature of human beings hasn't just changed dramatically over the last few decades. In other words, while there may be some contextual differences in the problems that we experience today, they are fundamentally the same problems that human beings have experienced over the millennia. This means that it may be wise to look for our answers in philosophies and traditions that have stood the test of time.

References

Balmford, A., Cole, L., Sandbrook, C., & Fisher, B. (2017). The environmental footprints of conservationists, economists and medics compared. *Biological Conservation, 214*, 260–269. https://doi.org/10.1016/j.biocon.2017.07.035

Baron-Cohen, S., Leslie, A. M., & Frith, U. (1985). Does the autistic child have a "theory of mind"? *Cognition, 21*(1), 37–46.

Baron, S. W. (2003). Self-control, social consequences, and criminal behavior: Street youth and the general theory of crime. *Journal of Research in Crime and Delinquency, 40*(4), 403–425.

Big Banks Accused of Climate Hypocrisy. (2020, July 7). *Financial Review*.

Bergsma, A., & Ardelt, M. (2012). Self-reported wisdom and happiness: An empirical investigation. *Journal of Happiness Studies, 13*(3), 481–499.

Berkovich-Ohana, A. (2017). A case study of a meditation-induced altered state: increased overall gamma synchronization. *Phenomenology and the Cognitive Sciences, 16*(1), 91–106.

Bronkhorst, J. (2011). *Karma*. University of Hawaii Press.

Ceci, M. W., & Kumar, V. (2016). A correlational study of creativity, happiness, motivation, and stress from creative pursuits. *Journal of Happiness Studies, 17*(2), 609–626.

Chatterjee, S., & Datta, D. (2016). *An introduction to Indian philosophy*. Motilal Banarsidass.

Chinmayananda, S. (2014). *Taittiriya Upanishad*. Central Chinmaya Mission Trust.

Condon, P., & Feldman Barrett, L. (2013). Conceptualizing and experiencing compassion. *Emotion, 13*(5), 817.

Correia, I., Salvado, S., & Alves, H. V. (2016). Belief in a just world and self-efficacy to promote justice in the world predict helping attitudes, but only among volunteers. *The Spanish Journal of Psychology, 19*.

Correia, I., & Vala, J. (2004). Belief in a just world, subjective well-being and trust of young adults. In *The justice motive in adolescence and young adulthood* (pp. 99–114). Routledge.

Coutinho, J. F., Fernandesl, S. V., Soares, J. M., Maia, L., Gonçalves, Ó. F., & Sampaio, A. (2016). Default mode network dissociation in depressive and anxiety states. *Brain Imaging and Behavior, 10*(1), 147–157.

Csikszentmihalyi, M. (1997). Happiness and creativity. *The Futurist, 31*(5), S8.

de Waal, F. (2007). *Chimpanzee politics: Power and sex among apes*. John Hopkins University Press.

Dillard, A. J., Midboe, A. M., & Klein, W. M. (2009). The dark side of optimism: Unrealistic optimism about problems with alcohol predicts subsequent negative event experiences. *Personality and Social Psychology Bulletin, 35*(11), 1540–1550.

Ehrenreich, B. (2009). *Bright-sided: How positive thinking is undermined America*. Metropolitan Books.

Facione, P. A., Scherer, D., & Attig, T. (1978). *Values and society an introduction to ethics and social philosophy*.

Fløistad, G. (2014). *Ethics or moral philosophy*. Springer.

Friedman, M. (1962/2009). *Capitalism and freedom*: University of Chicago press.

Friedman, M. (1970, September 13). The social responsibility of business is to increase its profits. *The New York Times Magazine*.

Furnham, A., Treglown, L., Hyde, G., & Trickey, G. (2016). The Bright and Dark side of altruism: Demographic, personality traits, and disorders associated with altruism. *Journal of Business Ethics, 134*(3), 359–368. https://doi.org/10.1007/s10551-014-2435-x

Gallagher, H. L., & Frith, C. D. (2003). Functional imaging of 'theory of mind.' *Trends in Cognitive Sciences, 7*(2), 77–83.

Gau, J. M., & Brunson, R. K. (2015). Procedural injustice, lost legitimacy, and self-help: Young males' adaptations to perceived unfairness in urban policing tactics. *Journal of Contemporary Criminal Justice, 31*(2), 132–150.

Goetz, J. L., Keltner, D., & Simon-Thomas, E. (2010). Compassion: An evolutionary analysis and empirical review. *Psychological Bulletin, 136*(3), 351.

Grubbs, J. B., Warmke, B., Tosi, J., James, A. S., & Campbell, W. K. (2019). Moral grandstanding in public discourse: Status-seeking motives as a potential explanatory mechanism in predicting conflict. *PloS one, 14*(10), e0223749.

Igou, E. R., Blake, A. A., & Bless, H. (2021). Just-world beliefs increase helping intentions via meaning and affect. *Journal of Happiness Studies, 22*(5), 2235–2253.

Imperatori, C., Farina, B., Adenzato, M., Valenti, E. M., Murgia, C., Della Marca, G., et al. (2019). Default mode network alterations in individuals with high-trait-anxiety: an EEG functional connectivity study. *Journal of Affective Disorders, 246*, 611–618.

Jacques, M. (2004). The death of intimacy. *The Guardian*, 18.

Kanada, M. Vaisheshika Sutras. https://sa.wikisource.org/wiki/%E0%A4%B5% E0%A5%88%E0%A4%B6%E0%A5%87%E0%A4%B7%E0%A4%BF%E0%A4%95% E0%A4%B8%E0%A5%82%E0%A4%A4%E0%A5%8D%E0%A4%B0%E0%A4% AE%E0%A5%8D.

Kasser, T., & Ryan, R. M. (1993). A dark side of the American dream: Correlates of financial success as a central life aspiration. *Journal of Personality and Social Psychology, 65*(2), 410.

Kaufman, M. (2005). Meditation gives brain a charge, study finds. *Washington Post, 3*

Keith, A. B. (1925). *The religion and philosophy of the Veda and Upanishads* (Vol. 31). Harvard University Press.

Lerner, M. J. (1980). *The belief in a just world: A fundamental delusion.* Springer.

Lewis, C. (2016). Inequality, incentives, criminality, and blame. *Legal Theory, 22*(2), 153–180.

Liang, C. T., & Borders, A. (2012). Beliefs in an unjust world mediate the associations between perceived ethnic discrimination and psychological functioning. *Personality and Individual Differences, 53*(4), 528–533.

Mehta, A. J. (2011). *Védic Dharma.* www.free-ebooks.net.

Miller, D. T. (2001). The norm of self-interest. *The next phase of business ethics: Integrating psychology and ethics.*

Murphy, R. (2019, August 02). There's no hypocrite like a rich, jet-setting anti-global-warming one. *National Post.* https://nationalpost.com/opinion/rex-murphy-theres-no-hypocritelike-a-rich-jet-setting-anti-global-warming-one.

Nudelman, G., & Otto, K. (2021). Personal Belief in a Just World and Conscientiousness: A meta-analysis, facet-level examination, and mediation model. *British Journal of Psychology, 112*(1), 92–119.

Nussbaum, M. (1996). Compassion: The basic social emotion. *Social Philosophy and Policy, 13*(1), 27–58.

Oakley, B., Knafo, A., Madhavan, G., & Wilson, D. S. (2011). *Pathological altruism.* Oxford University Press.

Passmore, J. A. (2004). Contemporary Concepts of Philosophy. In *Language, Meaning, Interpretation* (pp. 11–44). Springer.

Peterson, J. B. (2018). *12 rules for life: An antidote to chaos.* Penguin.

Piccardi, L., & Masse, W. B. (2007). Myth and geology. In *Geological Society of London.*

Raichle, M. E. (2015). The brain's default mode network. *Annual Review of Neuroscience, 38*, 433–447.

Ryan, W., & Pitman, W. (2000). *Noah's Flood: The new scientific discoveries about the event that changed history.* Simon and Schuster.

Sachs, J. D. (2019). Addiction and unhappiness in America. *World Happiness Report, 2019*, 122–131.

Saito, K. (2015). Impure altruism and impure selfishness. *Journal of Economic Theory, 158*, 336–370.

Shankaracharya, A. (1981). Vivekachudamani. *Mumbai: Khemraj Shrikrishnadass.*

Shepperd, J. A., Waters, E. A., Weinstein, N. D., & Klein, W. M. (2015). A primer on unrealistic optimism. *Current Directions in Psychological Science, 24*(3), 232–237.

Smith, A. (1776/1937). *An inquiry into the nature and causes of the wealth of nations.* Random House.

Stapleton, P., Dispenza, J., McGill, S., Sabot, D., Peach, M., & Raynor, D. (2020). Large effects of brief meditation intervention on EEG spectra in meditation novices. *IBRO Reports, 9*, 290–301.

Tosi, J., & Warmke, B. (2016). Moral grandstanding. *Philosophy & Public Affairs, 44*(3), 197–217.

Upenieks, L., Sendroiu, I., Levi, R., & Hagan, J. (2021). Beliefs about Legality and Benefits for Mental Health. *Journal of Health and Social Behavior*, 00221465211046359.

Vialatte, F. B., Bakardjian, H., Prasad, R., & Cichocki, A. (2009). EEG paroxysmal gamma waves during Bhramari Pranayama: a yoga breathing technique. *Consciousness and Cognition, 18*(4), 977–988.

White, C. J., Norenzayan, A., & Schaller, M. (2019). The content and correlates of belief in Karma across cultures. *Personality and Social Psychology Bulletin, 45*(8), 1184–1201.

Whitfield-Gabrieli, S., & Ford, J. M. (2012). Default mode network activity and connectivity in psychopathology. *Annual Review of Clinical Psychology, 8*, 49–76.

Whitmarsh, L., Capstick, S., Moore, I., Köhler, J., & Le Quéré, C. (2020). Use of aviation by climate change researchers: Structural influences, personal attitudes, and information provision. *Global Environmental Change, 65*. https://doi.org/10.1016/j.gloenvcha.2020.102184

Zhao, X.-H., Wang, P.-J., Li, C.-B., Hu, Z.-H., Xi, Q., Wu, W.-Y., et al. (2007). Altered default mode network activity in patient with anxiety disorders: An fMRI study. *European Journal of Radiology, 63*(3), 373–378.

CHAPTER 3

Uniqueness of the Dharmic Tradition

3.1 WHEN THE GODDESS OF WEALTH LEAVES YOU

In several Hindu *purāṇas*, there is the mention of a great sage named Durvāsā. His stature was such that everyone—from the *devas* (gods), asūras (demons) to human beings—revered him. Durvāsā was known for his extremely short temper. The literal meaning of his name is "one who is difficult to live with."

The Vishnū Pūrāna narrates that Durvāsā once decided to visit the *Swargaloka*. *Swargaloka* is often incorrectly translated as heaven in English; *Swargaloka* is just one of the fourteen dimensions of existence and is supposed to be two levels above *Bhuloka* the dimension where human beings reside with all other beings.

In any case, on reaching *Swargaloka,* Durvāsā visited god Indra, who presides over the *Swargaloka*. Indra at the time was in the company of Rambha, a celestial nymph. When Indra saw Durvāsā, he bowed at the feet of the revered sage, but soon got distracted by the seductiveness of Rambha. When Durvāsā gifted Indra, he politely accepted it but then casually threw it by the side. This discourtesy made Durvāsā furious. The enraged sage then cursed Indra.

> Indra! It is such a shame that you are distracted while sitting on the throne. You are so enticed by the sensuality of your nymphs that you do not even

P. Mishra and S. Kalagnanam, *Managing by Dharma*, Palgrave Studies in Workplace Spirituality and Fulfillment, https://doi.org/10.1007/978-3-030-90669-6_3

properly respect the sages anymore. It is clear that power has corrupted your mind. You do not deserve to be a king. I curse you that you will lose all your prosperity!

Durvāsā's curse turned Indra into a pauper. He lost all his wealth and the glamour that came from his position. Depressed with the turn of fate, the remorseful Indra went to the sage Nārada for help. Nārada said, he could not reverse Durvāsā's curse, and he should pray to god Brahmā, the creator of the world. Indra satisfied Brahmā with his prayers, who then took him to the supreme God, Vishnū. On hearing Indra's story, He said, "Even I cannot help you. Goddess Lakshmi, the goddess of wealth and prosperity has left you because of the transgression of you having offended an elderly sage. You should pray to Lakshmi."

Indra then performed deep sādhanā (concentrated spiritual practice) in the worship of Lakshmi. After a long period of sādhanā, Lakshmi was pleased with Indra. She told Indra that she couldn't reverse Durvāsā's curse, but she will bring back the wealth consciousness in Indra, which will help him face the challenges with fortitude.

The grateful Indra continued his sādhanā daily. Soon sage Durvāsā also noticed the positive changes in Indra. He forgave Indra, and finally, Indra regained all that he had lost.

3.2   THE PARADOX OF WEALTH

Everyone wants to get wealthy. This is not surprising, because wealth equates to an abundance of material comforts. When people have a lot of money, they do not have to worry about their basic needs of food, water, and shelter, and can instead enjoy the comfort and status associated with the luxurious versions of the same. The abundance of money brings with it tremendous amounts of freedom, which permits people to invest their energies in passions that excite them. More importantly, money also allows us the privilege of helping others and supporting causes that can enhance happiness in the world.

The truth is that only a small percentage of people are truly wealthy, although almost all of humanity aspires to be one. Becoming wealthy is not easy. It would be especially difficult—or even impossible—as long as people harbor negative beliefs about wealth. For example, the abundance of money is often associated with greed and corruption. Many religious people tend to view money as un-spiritual. Many people while personally aspiring for money also believe that money is the root of all evil (Tang et al., 2011; Wright et al., 2001). Is money is the root of evil or is it the other way round (Kiyotaki & Moore, 2002)? These are interesting questions for philosophical and scientific exploration, but they are unlikely to help build wealth.

People possess varied conscious and implicit beliefs about money (John-Henderson et al., 2013; Li-Ping Tang et al., 2000; Mitchell & Mickel, 1999; Roberts & Jones, 2001; Tang, 1992; Tang & Chen, 2008), which then impacts their motivation, behaviors, and even the satisfaction they derive from their jobs.

Negative beliefs and attitudes about money are not the only hindrances to making money. Often people possess the appropriate belief sets but lack the discipline that is critical to earning wealth and preserving it. In the story that we started this chapter with, Indra had all the requisite qualifications to attain the coveted position of being the king of *Swargaloka*. However, he lost all of his prosperity when he allowed the abundance and the associated luxuries to change him into an indolent and profligate god. Wealth indeed has the potential to change the way we think, feel, and act. Unfortunately, this change is not always in a desirable direction.

The psychological malaise of affluenza—a portmanteau of the words, affluence, and influenza—is not just a cultural criticism of wealth but also a phenomenon that has been empirically observed by researchers (De Graaf, 2002; De Graaf et al., 2014). It is not uncommon for wealthy young people to lack motivation, engage in substance abuse, and wallow in indulgence while simultaneously experiencing a lack of real connectedness with other human beings (Luthar, 2003). Research conducted by Michael Kraus and his colleagues shows that money and social class affect the level of empathy and compassion that people experience and express in their social relationships (Kraus et al., 2010; Stellar et al., 2012). In a highly cited research paper that included a series of seven studies, researchers found that wealthy, upper-class people not only endorsed beliefs that greed is good but also were more likely to lie and cheat in economic games and cut people off when driving (Piff et al., 2012).

3.3 Philosophies for Curbing Greed

Money is a double-edged sword. On the one hand, it is like a genie in a bottle, that can make many—if not all—of our dreams come true. On the other hand, it also appears to be like Satan incarnate that promises unimaginable gratification but who takes our soul in exchange for trifling pleasures.

The above metaphors are, of course, not from the Hindu tradition, but they do illustrate the love-hate relationship that many people have with money. It is no wonder then that extensive philosophies have developed to contain the power of money. In this section, we briefly discuss some of these paradigms that have also entered the business ethics literature.

Postmaterialism

The most dominant paradigm within the business ethics literature is perhaps the postmaterialist paradigm. If the world of business has primarily functioned embracing materialistic values and goals focused on prosperity, profits, possessions, and social status (Kasser, 2016), the logical alternative to it would be one that rejects them. Postmaterialism does exactly that. Developed by Inglehart (1971, 1977), it is a system of ideals that denounces all materialistic pursuits and instead celebrates non-material goals, such as self-expression, social equity, gender equality, community orientation, and environmentalism. Some may argue that postmaterialism does not reject materialistic values altogether and only rejects them as being the ultimate aims of human beings (and businesses). Either way, when we embrace postmaterialist values, the expectation is that it will help us "overcome the inclination to accept unethical organizational actions that are generally associated with materialist values" (Giacalone et al., 2008, p. 505).

Postmaterialist values are laudable, but that does not mean that they are above criticism. Abramson (2011) has summarized many critiques and counter-critiques to the postmaterialism thesis. The postmaterialist values may be especially problematic in the world of business, as they tend to be more idealistic and less practical. They fall apart under the pressures of business. That is perhaps the reason why they haven't been attractive to ambitious businessmen, unless (paradoxically) they fulfill some of their materialistic goals. This leads to the current state of affairs where morality and ethics are things that are talked about a great deal but not practiced sufficiently. In businesses, this is what leads to the whitewashing of unethical business practices.

Communism/Socialism

If the materialistic pursuits of capitalism heighten greed and its associated evils, another valid alternative should be communism, or at least, its milder cousin, socialism. Both communism and socialism have their roots in the works of Karl Marx (2000) from the nineteenth century. Marx was unhappy with capitalism because he thought it created and aggravated class differences just like feudalism did during the pre-industrial period. Thus, while capitalism celebrates individualism, communism and socialism give utmost priority to the "collective good" that is realized by the redistribution of wealth through political and/or revolutionary means.

In the introduction to his short book on socialism, Newman (2020) describes that for more than a hundred years after Marx, many socialists (and communists) believed that there was no future of capitalism and it would soon be replaced by socialism (and communism). Things have, of course, changed dramatically over the last few decades, especially after the collapse of the former Soviet bloc, the forerunner of Marx's ideas.

A key problem with the communist and socialist worldviews is that it attempts to distribute resources equally, ignoring the varying contributions that different people make to the generation of wealth. This aspect was also illustrated in the opening story of Chapter 1 when the god Prabhās' wife insisted that the immortality milk from the *Kāmadhenū* cow be given to her human friend even if she hadn't earned it.

Both communism and socialistic philosophies endorse taking wealth from somebody who has earned it and redistributing it among those who haven't. There are certainly a few merits in communistic and socialistic philosophies, but history is proof that systems based on these philosophies haven't succeeded in curtailing greed. Instead, these philosophies created a "whole pathological system of communist tyranny" (Peterson, 2018, p. 155) that has killed at least 100 million people in its 100+ years of existence (Satter, 2017).

3.4 Religious Approaches to Curbing Greed

Postmaterialism, communism, and socialism are secular paradigms of business ethics. Seeing the failure of these paradigms, over the last decade scholars are starting to show increasing interest in spiritual- or religious-based ethical models of business (Bouckaert & Zsolnai, 2011;

Giacalone & Jurkiewicz, 2010; Karakas, 2010; Rocha & Pinheiro, 2021). This is certainly a desirable development in the field because religious traditions over the millennia have had some interesting and powerful perspectives on various dimensions of human life, including what ought to be human beings' relationship with wealth. In this section, we provide an overview of a few distinct religious paradigms that exist on how to curb greed.

The Abrahamic Approach

As briefly discussed in Chapter 1, wealth and greed aren't viewed in positive terms in Abrahamic religions. Although they vary in their emphasis (Bloch, 1984; Oka & Kuijt, 2014; Rosen, 2009), all three religions look down upon the pursuit of wealth, with the harshest condemnations existing within Christianity.

> No one can serve two masters. You cannot serve both God and money.— Matthew 6:24

> Those who trust in their riches will fall.—Proverbs 11:28

The approach here is essentially to create a sense of disgust and revulsion for greed, so people are not tempted to pursue it (Rosen, 2009). Looking at some of the verses in the James Bible, one also gets the impression that it creates a fear among the followers that the sin of coveting wealth would be punished in the harshest terms.

> Now listen, you rich people, weep and wail because of the misery that is coming on you. Your wealth has rotted, and moths have eaten your clothes. Your gold and silver are corroded. Their corrosion will testify against you and eat your flesh like fire.—James 5:1–3

The "Spiritual But Not Religious" Way

Incorporating religious ethics into the study of ethical ways of doing business can certainly be an extremely powerful and effective enterprise. However, the problem with religious-based ethics is that many religions have enormous historical baggage. In their quest for conversion, certain religious traditions have also caused the murders of millions of people over the millennia. Perhaps, this is the reason why mainstream scholars had largely avoided incorporating religious paradigms into business ethics. Some have proposed an alternative "spiritual but not religious" to disassociate with the dark side of religion (Giacalone & Jurkiewicz, 2010; Kolodinsky et al., 2008; Parsons, 2018). According to these thinkers, spirituality, in contrast to religion, is personal and has a deeper meaning of life without the negative baggage that comes from religion.

The notion of "spiritual but not religious" is not without problems either, because it ignores the question of why religion exists. Religions have existed across all cultures and seem to have an evolutionary basis (Wade, 2009). Why haven't people only been "spiritual but not religious" in the past? Why does a large part of the world population embrace religion even today in modern society? Religion is a big part of people's lives. It continues to influence their lives.

While there are similarities between religions, there also exist significant differences between them. Even if we focus on the common denominator of all religions, it is not always clear what needs to be subtracted from religion so that we are left with the idea of "spiritual but not religious." And after religion has been stripped of those indeterminate segments, would what is left be still attractive and impactful to people's lives? These are questions to which we do not have clear answers yet, but they are worth asking.

The Chārvāka *Way*

In the previous chapter, we briefly mentioned the Chārvāka school of thought, an atheistic philosophy within the Hindu tradition that vehemently denies the existence of any supernatural powers such as God(s). Etymologically, the word Chārvāka means "agreeable speech" or "sweet talkers." The school fell out of favor over time. However, there is a shloka (chant) within that tradition that describes in accurate detail the cause of our present suffering:

Yavan jivet sukham jivet, rinam kritva ghritam pibet |
Bhasmi bhutasya dehasya punaragmanam kritah ||

Just enjoy your life; seek comforts and luxuries even if you have to take a loan; follow this approach to life because you will die one day anyway and people will burn your body away.

The Chārvāka philosophy essentially says, "You only have one life to live. So, enjoy it fully by seeking material and sensual pleasures. If you cannot afford the luxuries of life, simply buy them on loan, but enjoy your life, because once you are dead, you will not be able to experience any of the pleasures anymore."

On the surface, the Chārvāka philosophy may make sense and be extremely attractive to many people. To a large extent, people in the modern world also tend to live their lives based on this premise. However, there are numerous problems with this hedonistic way of living. All hedonistic pleasures are fleeting; the pleasure one derives from sex, for example, lasts only for a short time. Howsoever, pleasurable a hedonistic act may have been, after some time one will always return to one's default level of happiness. In other words, if one hasn't developed the skill to be happy without the indulgence of material and sensual pleasures, then one will often find oneself in a state of happiness lacunae and will be perpetually seeking excitement without ever experiencing any lasting happiness. In the psychology literature, this has been referred to as being on a hedonic treadmill (Diener et al., 2009).

There are several other problems with the Chārvāka approach to life. For example, there will always be uncertainty about having regular access to materials or people that give hedonistic pleasure. In the rare situations where one does get access to an unlimited supply of hedonistic pleasures, one still pays a heavy price. As we discussed earlier in the chapter, addictions, loneliness, and lack of authentic relationships are common problems among many affluent people who suffer tremendously in their lives despite having constant access to all the hedonic pleasures of the world. The Chārvāka lifestyle, which has become so common in the modern world, always leaves a long trail of chaos and suffering behind it. One needs to look no further than the horribly messed-up lives and tragic suicidal deaths of many modern celebrities to realize the painful meaninglessness and emptiness that comes from choosing this philosophy of living.

The Buddhist Way

While the Chārvāka way of life promotes the indulgence of desires, Buddhism takes the exact opposite approach. Greed is not considered to be good within the Buddhist tradition. It is described as a poison of the mind. It is one of the three mental afflictions—the other two being hatred and delusion—that cause suffering. "Desire is the root of all suffering," is one of the basic premises of Buddhism (Epstein, 2005). And thus, it is recommended within the tradition to develop the ability to give up desires. Instead of hankering for a desirable future, the approach is to mindfully enjoy the here and now (Strosahl & Robinson, 2015).

Is there any validity in the Buddhist approach? The thousands of studies done on mindfulness meditation do show strong evidence of it having immense positive benefits on people's physical and psychological health (Creswell & Lindsay, 2014; Grossman et al., 2004). However, the question that also needs to be asked is, "Are these benefits the effect of the mindfulness meditation technique, or are they the effect of renouncing desire?" One may also ask, "Does mindfulness succeed in removing desire, or does it only lessen it?"

3.5   When Desire Isn't a Dirty Word: The Hindu Way

The Hindu tradition holds that hedonistic desires are not necessarily bad. They do not automatically induce suffering. From an evolutionary perspective as well, the pleasures we derive from food and sex are just in-built reward mechanisms that facilitate the survival of species. So if we all gave up the pursuit of hedonistic desires, human beings will likely go extinct within a couple of centuries.

As per the Hindu tradition, giving up desires can be a valid approach to achieving sustainable happiness. It is not uncommon to see greater tranquility in older adults, that's because age-related hormonal changes in the body cause a decline in the intensity of desires in people. Empirical research on the topic also confirms that there is a general trend of happiness increasing in adults with age, although it declines after a certain point when painful age-related ailments start arising in the body (Laaksonen, 2018).

When people give up hedonistic desires, there sure seems to be an increase in happiness, but the problem is that most people are both unwilling to and incapable of giving up their desires. Human beings generally do not give up on their desires until nature or circumstances force them to.

Shankara's Stand

The Hindu tradition holds that there is nothing immoral about wishing or striving for wealth. Instead, it recognizes and values the benefits that come from wealth. This might be because this religion developed in a region of the world that had enormous prosperity. According to the British economist Angus Maddison (2007), India's share of the world GDP was over 30% for most of the first millennium and started declining only after the Hindu kings became weak and the economy was taken over by Islamic invaders and later by the British colonialists.

Similar to the views of Aristotle (Raftari, 2015), the Hindu tradition also holds that happiness is the ultimate goal of all human beings. The tradition goes further in emphasizing that it is not only the ultimate goal of human beings but of all living beings. The hamsters' notion of happiness may be very different from the human beings' conception of it, but at a fundamental level, both are striving for a state of sustained pleasantness within them. The purpose of life is to flourish, whatever the life form.

Adi Shankaracharya (1910), the eighth-century Hindu saint whose commentaries on the Vedas and Upanishads are considered the golden standard said (p. 1):

Dvividho hi vedokto dharmah pravritilakshano nivritilakshanascha jagatah sthiti kāranam | Prāninam sākshat abhuydaya nihshreyasa hetuh …

Shankara's words can roughly be translated as follows:

According to the Vedas, as long as one is acting as per dharma, sustainability in the world (*jagatah sthiti kāranam*) can be achieved, irrespective of whether one is following (1) *pravritilakshana* (i.e., the path where you get yourself involved in the worldly affairs) or (2) *nivritilakshana* (i.e., the path where you get committed to spirituality). It is important to master dharma because all living creatures (*Prāninam sākshat*) ultimately want *Abhyudaya* and *Nihshreyasa*. As we have already explained in the previous chapter, *Abhyudaya* means the enhancement of happiness, and *Nihshreyasa* means the cessation of suffering.

In simple words, all living beings aspire for more happiness and less suffering, and these goals can be achieved sustainably by following the principles of dharma.

The Prayer of a Sage

May the Brahman make me wise... May my physical body be healthy... May Lakshmi... the goddess of wealth... bring to me ... an abundance of animals. May she bring me clothing, cows, food grains, and articles of drink. May she ensure a steady supply of these objects and may she nurture them for my use. ... May I be famous among men. May I be richer than the richest...

The above lines are taken from a translation of the Taittirīya Upanishad by Debroy and Debroy (2020). The Taittirīya Upanishad is a principal Upanishad and appears in the Yajurveda. The above lines present part of a prayer recited by the notable Vedic sage named, Yajnavalkya. We see in this prayer a list of things that the sage desires. There is a common belief that sages ought to have renounced all their desires. If desires were immoral and detrimental to spiritual development, why would a great sage such as Yajnavalkya have them included in his prayer?

3.6   THE PURUSHĀRTHA MODEL

The Hindu dharmic tradition holds that there is nothing intrinsically wrong with desires. Desires are integral to our existence and happiness. The tradition highlights four broad categories of desires and lists them as worthwhile goals of life. These goals are dharma, artha, kāma, and moksha. They are collectively called the purushārthas. These are legitimate goals for all human beings because they provide a sense of purpose and keep them happy.

Dharma

The first goal in the purushārtha system is dharma. Dharma is the goal of building the necessary discipline within oneself so that one can be successful and happy in life. Dharma is the goal of developing and strengthening the ability to delay gratification. Dharma is developing the abilities of meditation and concentration. Dharma is the goal of learning and internalizing the values that make people successful and retain that success for a long time. Dharma is the goal of developing a strong and flexible body so that one can accomplish difficult physical tasks, fight enemies, and also enjoy the pleasures of the body for a long time. Dharma is the goal of strengthening the logical, critical, and moral thinking skills that are so critical to making wise choices in life. Dharma is the goal of cultivating one's creativity so that one can enjoy the sublime pleasures of creating something new. Dharma is the goal of reinforcing one's strengths and mending one's weaknesses so that one can courageously face the varied challenges of life. Dharma is toughening oneself up for the exigencies of life. Dharma is developing a higher capacity for compassion. Dharma is harmonizing the important dimensions of the human personality.

Dharma essentially refers to building a strong foundation within oneself. It is akin to the necessity of a strong foundation while building a tall skyscraper; without it, the whole edifice will fall apart.

Artha

Artha is the goal of acquiring money. Artha is the goal of earning a higher salary. Artha is the wish of winning a lottery. Artha is the goal of possessing gold, diamonds, and other valuables. Artha is the goal of owning lands and expensive properties. Artha is the goal of owning copyrights and patents. Artha is the goal of receiving fat royalties. Artha is the goal of advancing in one's career. Artha is the goal of having a sizeable pension after retirement. Artha is the goal of having access to good medical care. Artha is the goal of acquiring more power. Artha is the goal of being famous.

The literal meaning of artha is "means of life." Artha refers to all those goals that enable the survival and thriving of human beings. Artha-related goals are valid goals of life because they provide the necessary resources for living a secured and comfortable life. Acquiring artha also provides a sense of accomplishment, which makes people happy. Artha allows us to take care of our family's needs. Artha enables us to help our friends. Artha provides us the resources to do good for society. For these reasons, there is nothing immoral in seeking artha.

Kāma

The next valid goal is kāma. Kāma refers to the goal of seeking physical and sensual pleasures. Kāma is the goal of enjoying tasty food. Kāma is the wish to enjoy intoxicating drinks. Kāma is the wish of wanting to stay under the warm sheets on a cold Winter morning. Kāma is cuddling up with one's lover. Kāma is having sex. Kāma is watching pornography. Essentially, kāma refers to all those pleasures that we experience through our physical sense organs.

The purushārtha system holds that it is not immoral to pursue kāma. This might seem contradictory to our criticism of the Charvaka school of thought, but we will explain the validity of kāma immediately after we list the last goal in the purushārtha system.

Moksha

The fourth valid goal of life is Moksha. Moksha is the goal of attaining freedom from all the suffering in the world, and not just in the short term, but permanently. Moksha is the goal of realizing one's true self. Moksha is the goal of connecting with God. From the perspective of karma and reincarnation, moksha is the goal of freeing oneself from the cycle of birth, death, and rebirth. If we use the language of the Buddhists, moksha is the goal of achieving nirvana. Moksha is the goal of reaching a state where one does not crave or cling to any of the lower goals of life (i.e., dharma, artha, and kāma).

Moksha is considered the supreme purushārtha. It is the most advanced goal and may not be suited for a large section of the population. Unlike dharma, which is considered an obligatory goal, moksha is more of an aspirational goal. People tend to pursue moksha only when they realize the futility of pursuing artha, kāma, and even dharma.

3.7   The Big Picture

When it comes to managing our desires and their extreme forms manifested in form of greed and lust, different traditions have proposed different solutions. The postmaterialism approach downplayed the importance of materialistic goals and tried to replace material needs with values that are supposed to be more noble and laudable. The communist approach managed greed by curtailing freedom, and by forcefully redistributing the rewards of competent and hardworking people among people who didn't earn those rewards. Most religions denounced desire. Sometimes they shamed people for having desires and at other times, they created fear in them by describing in vivid detail the horrible punishments that would be meted out to the sinners in their afterlife.

Then we also discussed the hedonistic approaches, such as the Chārvāka school of thought. These approaches tend to be skeptical of our ability to bring about any good in society. Thus, they recommended that we dive ourselves into the pool of sensual indulgence and forget about the problems of the world. Finally, the Buddhist approach, which did not shame people for their desires, but recommended people to forego their desires because of the suffering it caused in the present life.

All the above models attempted to tackle the problem in a piecemeal fashion like the blind men in the Hindu parable of the Blind Men and an Elephant. For those who might not know the story, the parable describes a group of blind men who come across an elephant, an animal that they had never been exposed to before. They tried to make sense of the animal by touching its body. Depending on the part they touched, they described the elephant as a tree trunk (for the leg), fan (for the ear), wall (for the torso), rope (for the tail), and a large snake (for the trunk).

There is a lot of variety in the existing approaches to tackling the dark side of greed. However, leaving aside purushārtha approach, they all tend to be unidimensional in their approaches. The purushārtha model did not attempt to downplay the importance of desires nor did it shame people for their desires. It also did not suggest idealistic and impractical approaches to curtailing one's desire. Nor did it give up on the challenges of life and recommend a life, where one took every possible opportunity to drown oneself in sensual pleasures.

The Purushārtha model recognized that the pursuit of wealth (artha) and pleasures (kāma) were valid desires because they are fundamental to our existence. However, it also did not ignore the dangers associated with the pursuit of wealth and pleasures, and it identified dharma as another valid goal because of its ability to moderate the dark sides of artha and kāma while simultaneously enhancing their bright side. Dharma makes people more disciplined, which then increases the probability that they will succeed in attaining their goals of artha and kāma.

The greatest insight of the purushārtha model is illustrated in Fig. 3.1. It shows that the model is not just an assemblage of discrete goals of life. Rather, it prescribes that the goals be pursued in a specific sequence. Dharma should be pursued first because it builds the foundational discipline that makes the other goals attainable, and on attainment, retainable. Dharma provides the discipline that makes artha possible, and artha provides the means to buy kāma and enjoy it for a longer time.

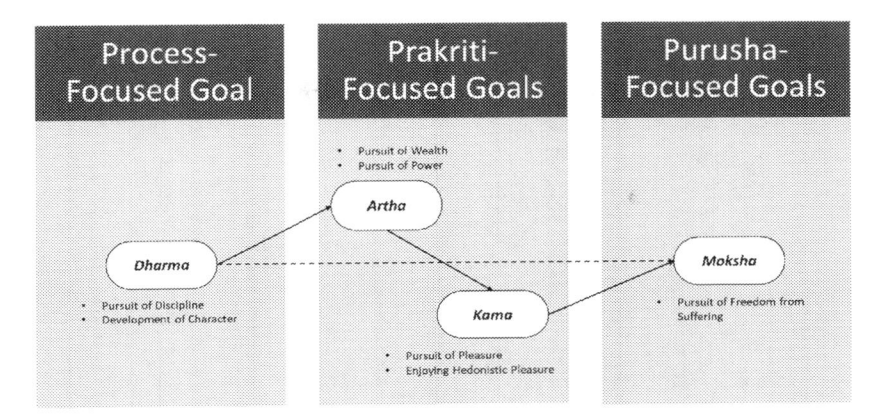

Fig. 3.1 The Purushārtha model

In the opening story of this chapter, we saw, how Indra succeed in becoming the king of a heavenly plane based on the merits of his karma. However, he started ignoring the dimension of the dharma after he successfully got the coveted throne and got more focused on the alluring pleasures (kāma) of the heavenly realm, and that caused his downfall. He lost all his wealth and along with it the access to all the pleasures that he had become accustomed to. As per the story, he got back his kingdom only after he rebuilt his discipline of dharma by performing penances and doing the sadhana of goddess Lakshmi, the goddess of wealth. The story illustrates that you cannot get artha (wealth), and if you do, you cannot retain it for long if you do not have the discipline that is built through dharma.

Lastly, the purushārtha model also recognizes the limits of artha and kāma. Similar to the Buddhist perspective, it holds that materialistic pursuits and sensual pleasures, after a certain point, do not give the deep and lasting sense of happiness that human beings desire. Thus, it is not uncommon for people to realize the futility of pursuing artha and kāma after they have had the opportunity to indulge in them for a while. It is then that they get a genuine motivation to reorient themselves towards moksha.

This also corresponds perfectly well with the four āshramās (stages) of human life. Illustrated in Fig. 3.2, the āshrama model recommends that people invest in different purushārthas at different stages of life. The

Fig. 3.2   The four stages of life

Brahmacharya āshrama, characterized by voluntary celibacy, learning, and the building of different skills, is the stage where one focuses on pursuing dharma. One also consciously avoids the pursuit of pleasure, because of the hindrance it creates in the path of dharma. When the experienced and accomplished Indra slips out of dharma by getting carried away by kāma, one can imagine the extent of challenge for youngsters of simultaneously pursuing dharma and kāma. Unfortunately, such simultaneous pursuits have become the norm in today's world, and one can see the negative consequences of it in form of the highest ever levels of anxiety, depression, and suicidal thoughts among the youth (Beiter et al., 2015; Eisenberg et al., 2007; Fernandes et al., 2018; Kendall et al., 2010; Liu et al., 2019; Mortier et al., 2018).

Only after a person has invested sufficient time in building the discipline of dharma is it recommended that she/he enter the Grihastha stage, where the person gets married, focuses on earning money (artha) for his family, and enjoys the pleasures of marital life (kāma).

The third stage is referred to as the Vanaprastha ashrama, which could be described as the post-retirement stage where one hands over responsibilities to the future generation, thereby giving himself/herself the necessary mental space of not continuing to mindlessly pursue artha and kāma. This space then helps get people ready for the last stage of Sanyāsa āshrama, where they focus exclusively on the pursuit of moksha. We won't delve too much into the Moksha goal in our book, because it is primarily spiritual in nature, and our book is focused more on addressing the clear and present needs of the human world.

The problem of the existing models of ethics is that they have ignored the truth that human beings are multi-dimensional who cannot be forced-fit into singular categories. They also cannot be forced to adopt one particular way of life even if that particular way of life promises to be beneficial to self, society, and the environment.

The purushārtha approach, instead of downplaying certain desires or chastising them, identified all the desires and created a model of prioritization that is not based on some arbitrary moral parameter but on the very practical premise that attainment of the first purushārtha makes it easier for the second purushārtha to be achieved, and so on. Without a strong foundation of dharma, it will be difficult to attain artha; without artha it will be difficult to attain and retain kāma. Without enough artha, we won't be able to buy or attract kāma or pleasures in our life. And lastly, unless we get disillusioned by the mindless striving of artha and kāma, we will never genuinely work in the direction of moksha.

3.8   Conclusion

The hedonistic orientation to living that is dominant today (also, recommended in the Chārvāka approach) is not only problematic at the individual level, but it also destroys civilizations. For example, the once-powerful and prosperous Roman civilization fell apart once the rulers and populace of Rome got into hedonistic depravity (Morley, 2004). Valmiki's Ramayana also provides an excellent example of such a collapse. Specifically, the fifth section of the book, i.e., Sundara Kanda, describes in glorious detail the richness and prosperity of Lanka, the capital of the Asura king, Ravana. However, Ravana's Lanka got destroyed because it was a state that pursued artha and kāma at the cost of dharma. Could something similar happen to the prosperous world that we live in today?

References

Abramson, P. R. (2011). Critiques and counter-critiques of the postmaterialism thesis: Thirty-four years of debate. UC Irvine, CSD Working Papers. https://escholarship.org/uc/item/3f72v9q4.

Beiter, R., Nash, R., McCrady, M., Rhoades, D., Linscomb, M., Clarahan, M., & Sammut, S. (2015). The prevalence and correlates of depression, anxiety, and stress in a sample of college students. *Journal of affective disorders, 173*, 90–96.

Bloch, A. P. (1984). *A book of Jewish ethical concepts: Biblical and postbiblical.* KTAV Publishing House, Inc.

Bouckaert, L., & Zsolnai, L. (2011). Spirituality and business. In *Handbook of spirituality and business* (pp. 3–8). Springer.

Creswell, J. D., & Lindsay, E. K. (2014). How does mindfulness training affect health? A mindfulness stress buffering account. *Current Directions in Psychological Science, 23*(6), 401–407.

De Graaf, J. (2002). Affluenza: The all-consuming epidemic. *Environmental Management and Health.*

De Graaf, J., Wann, D., & Naylor, T. H. (2014). *Affluenza: How overconsumption is killing us—And how to fight back.* Berrett-Koehler Publishers.

Debroy, B., & Debroy, D. (2020). *The upanishads.* Books for All.

Diener, E., Lucas, R. E., & Scollon, C. N. (2009). Beyond the hedonic treadmill: Revising the adaptation theory of well-being. In *The science of well-being* (pp. 103–118). Springer.

Eisenberg, D., Gollust, S. E., Golberstein, E., & Hefner, J. L. (2007). Prevalence and correlates of depression, anxiety, and suicidality among university students. *American Journal of Orthopsychiatry, 77*(4), 534–542.

Epstein, M. (2005). *Open to desire: The truth about what the Buddha taught.* Gotham Books.

Fernandes, M. A., Vieira, F. E. R., Silva, J. S., Avelino, F. V. S. D., & Santos, J. D. M. (2018). Prevalence of anxious and depressive symptoms in college students of a public institution. *Revista Brasileira De Enfermagem, 71,* 2169–2175.

Giacalone, R. A., & Jurkiewicz, C. L. (2010). The science of workplace spirituality. In *Handbook of workplace spirituality and organizational performance* (pp. 19–42). Routledge.

Giacalone, R. A., Jurkiewicz, C. L., & Deckop, J. R. (2008). On ethics and social responsibility: The impact of materialism, postmaterialism, and hope. *Human Relations, 61*(4), 483–514.

Grossman, P., Niemann, L., Schmidt, S., & Walach, H. (2004). Mindfulness-based stress reduction and health benefits: A meta-analysis. *Journal of Psychosomatic Research, 57*(1), 35–43.

Inglehart, R. (1971). The silent revolution in Europe: Intergenerational change in post-industrial societies. *American Political Science Review, 65*(4), 991–1017.

Inglehart, R. (1977). *The silent revolution: Changing values and political styles among western publics.* Princeton University Press.

John-Henderson, N., Jacobs, E. G., Mendoza-Denton, R., & Francis, D. D. (2013). Wealth, health, and the moderating role of implicit social class bias. *Annals of Behavioral Medicine, 45*(2), 173–179.

Karakas, F. (2010). Spirituality and performance in organizations: A literature review. *Journal of Business Ethics, 94*(1), 89–106.

Kasser, T. (2016). Materialistic values and goals. *Annual Review of Psychology, 67*, 489–514.

Kendall, P. C., Compton, S. N., Walkup, J. T., Birmaher, B., Albano, A. M., Sherrill, J., Ginsburg, G., Rynn, M., McCracken, J., Gosch, E., & Keeton, C. (2010). Clinical characteristics of anxiety disordered youth. *Journal of anxiety disorders, 24*(3), 360–365.

Kiyotaki, N., & Moore, J. (2002). Evil is the root of all money. *American Economic Review, 92*(2), 62–66.

Kolodinsky, R. W., Giacalone, R. A., & Jurkiewicz, C. L. (2008). Workplace values and outcomes: Exploring personal, organizational, and interactive workplace spirituality. *Journal of Business Ethics, 81*(2), 465–480.

Kraus, M. W., Côté, S., & Keltner, D. (2010). Social class, contextualism, and empathic accuracy. *Psychological Science, 21*(11), 1716–1723.

Laaksonen, S. (2018). A research note: Happiness by age is more complex than U-shaped. *Journal of Happiness Studies, 19*(2), 471–482.

Li-Ping Tang, T., Kim, J. K., & Shin-Hsiung Tang, D. (2000). Does attitude toward money moderate the relationship between intrinsic job satisfaction and voluntary turnover? *Human Relations, 53*(2), 213–245.

Liu, C. H., Stevens, C., Wong, S. H., Yasui, M., & Chen, J. A. (2019). The prevalence and predictors of mental health diagnoses and suicide among US college students: Implications for addressing disparities in service use. *Depression and Anxiety, 36*(1), 8–17.

Luthar, S. S. (2003). The culture of affluence: Psychological costs of material wealth. *Child Development, 74*(6), 1581–1593. https://doi.org/10.1046/j.1467-8624.2003.00625.x

Maddison, A. (2007). *Contours of the world economy 1-2030 AD: Essays in macroeconomic history*. Oxford University Press.

Marx, K. (2000). *Karl Marx: Selected writings*. Oxford University Press.

Mitchell, T. R., & Mickel, A. E. (1999). The meaning of money: An individual-difference perspective. *Academy of Management Review, 24*(3), 568–578.

Morley, N. (2004). Decadence as a theory of history. *New Literary History, 35*(4), 573–585.

Mortier, P., Cuijpers, P., Kiekens, G., Auerbach, R. P., Demyttenaere, K., Green, J. G., Kessler, R. C., Nock, M. K., & Bruffaerts, R. (2018). The prevalence of suicidal thoughts and behaviours among college students: A meta-analysis. *Psychological medicine, 48*(4), 554–565.

Newman, M. (2020). *Socialism: A very short introduction*. Oxford University Press.

Oka, R., & Kuijt, I. (2014). Greed is bad, neutral, and good: A historical perspective on excessive accumulation and consumption. *Economic Anthropology, 1*(1), 30–48.

Parsons, W. B. (2018). *Being spiritual but not religious: Past, present, future (s)*. Routledge.

Peterson, J. B. (2018). *12 rules for life: An antidote to chaos*. Penguin UK.

Piff, P. K., Stancato, D. M., Côté, S., Mendoza-Denton, R., & Keltner, D. (2012). Higher social class predicts increased unethical behavior. *Proceedings of the National Academy of Sciences, 109*(11), 4086–4091.

Raftari, H. (2015). Happiness in view of Aristotle and Avicenna. *International Journal of Social Science and Humanity, 5*(8), 714.

Roberts, J. A., & Jones, E. (2001). Money attitudes, credit card use, and compulsive buying among American college students. *Journal of Consumer Affairs, 35*(2), 213–240.

Rocha, R. G., & Pinheiro, P. G. (2021). Organizational spirituality: Concept and perspectives. *Journal of Business Ethics, 171*(2), 241–252.

Rosen, J. (2009). Greed in Jewish Lore. In *Greed* (pp. 112–122). Springer.

Satter, D. (2017). 100 years of communism—And 100 million dead. *Wall Street Journal, 6*.

Shankaracharya, A. (1910). *The Bhagavad Gita Bhasya* (Vol. 1). Sri Vani Vilas Presss.

Stellar, J. E., Manzo, V. M., Kraus, M. W., & Keltner, D. (2012). Class and compassion: Socioeconomic factors predict responses to suffering. *Emotion, 12*(3), 449.

Strosahl, K. D., & Robinson, P. J. (2015). *In this moment: Five steps to transcending stress using mindfulness and neuroscience*. New Harbinger Publications.

Tang, T. L.-P. (1992). The meaning of money revisited. *Journal of Organizational Behavior*, 197–202.

Tang, T. L.-P., & Chen, Y.-J. (2008). Intelligence vs. wisdom: The love of money, Machiavellianism, and unethical behavior across college major and gender. *Journal of Business Ethics, 82*(1), 1–26.

Tang, T. L. P., Sutarso, T., Ansari, M. A., Lim, V. K., Teo, T. S., Arias-Galicia, F., Garber, I., Vlerick, P., Akande, A., Allen, M. W., & Alzubaidi, A. S. (2011). The love of money is the root of all evil: Pay satisfaction and CPI as moderators. In *Academy of management proceedings, 2011* (Vol. 2011, No. 1, pp. 1–6). Academy of Management Briarcliff Manor.

Wade, N. (2009). *The faith instinct: How religion evolved and why it endures*. Penguin.

Wright, J. P., Cullen, F. T., Agnew, R. S., & Brezina, T. (2001). "The root of all evil"? An exploratory study of money and delinquent involvement. *Justice Quarterly, 18*(2), 239–268.

CHAPTER 4

Dharmic Leadership

4.1 LAKSHMI'S CHOICE

Samudra Manthan (or the churning of the milk ocean) is a metaphorical event that is described in several Puranas (e.g., the Bhagavata Purana, Mahabharata, Vishnu Purana, Kurma Purana, Padma Purana Purana). The story goes that the asuras (or the demons) and the devas (or the gods) were in a constant fight with each other. Both sides used to suffer heavy losses. Both sides were wishing for the nectar that would make them immortal. This would help them pursue their goals of power and pleasure without any obstacles.

A certain turn of events led them to choose to collaborate to churn the celestial milk ocean (a metaphor for the milky way). The churning was supposed to bring to the surface unimaginable treasures, and most importantly, the nectar to immortality (amrit). But churning a huge ocean was an impossible task without the appropriate tools. They used the celestial Mandara mountain as the churning rod and Vasuki (the snake on Shiva's neck) as the churning rope.

The devas and asuras found it very difficult to churn the ocean because the Mandara mountain would start slipping off the Vasuki rope into the deep ocean. Vishnu came to the rescue. He took the form of a huge tortoise and placed himself under the Mandara mountain. With there being a proper base now, the churning continued without much difficulty.

P. Mishra and S. Kalagnanam, *Managing by Dharma*, Palgrave Studies in Workplace Spirituality and Fulfillment, https://doi.org/10.1007/978-3-030-90669-6_4

But even after a long time of churning, no treasure showed up on the surface. The churners started getting impatient, especially the asuras. The asuras were impatient, to begin with, but they were also working under more difficult conditions than the devas. Specifically, they were holding the head side of the snake that was being used for churning, which meant that they had to work under the difficult condition of being exposed to all the venom leaking out of Vasuki.

Eons went by without much happening and then suddenly treasures started showing up on the surface of the ocean. Some of the notable things that emerged were Kaustubha (a divine jewel), the wish-fulfilling cow named Kamadhenu, Amrita (nectar), Halahala (extremely toxic poison), many Apsaras (divine nymphs) such as Rambha, Menaka, etc., Dhanvantari (the god of medicine), and the goddess of wealth, Lakshmi.

These valuables were claimed up by different devas and asuras. A fight erupted over the nectar. Nobody wanted the Halahala poison, but it could not be left out in the open because of its extreme toxicity. So, Shiva offered to drink it. Because of his yogic powers, the lethal poison didn't kill him but it turned his throat blue (this got him the name, Neelakanth, or literally, the one with the blue throat).

When Lakshmi emerged from the ocean, the story goes that all devas and asuras rushed to seek her. However, Lakshmi had an independent personality. She would only go to the one she chose. She looked around and chose the god Vishnu, who, unlike the other gods, was not engulfed by greed. According to the Puranas, Lakshmi said, she chose Vishnu because of his abundance mentality and he not hankering after the treasures that emerged from the ocean.

4.2   BUSINESS LESSONS

Like all other stories in the Puranas, the Samudra Manthan story is a metaphor for the various dimensions of the dhārmic philosophy. The story, specifically, is an excellent metaphor for the world of work and provides valuable insights about what helps people succeed in that world.

Managing Processes

In the last chapter, we discussed the four purushārthas or the four goals worth pursuing. At an even broader level, everyone essentially has two goals. The first is to live forever. At a practical level, we know immortality is impossible, but we all (including plants and animals) wish to live as long a life as possible. The only exception to our first goal is the condition where we are in pain, which is when we might wish to die sooner to free ourselves from the pain. The second goal is happiness. As we have already discussed in the previous chapter, this too is a universal goal for all living creatures. It makes sense to live a long life only when we are happy and living without pain. That the devas and asuras were seeking the nectar is an illustration of these two fundamental goals of life. Nectar would give them immortality, which then would allow them to pursue what they valued indefinitely.

The second lesson from the story is that we need to be able to cooperate and collaborate with others to get what we value. As per the story, the devas and asuras were initially in constant fights with each other. Such an environment where we are in constant combat with each other is not conducive for us to realize our goals. It was only after the devas and asuras decided to collaborate that they could engage in the complex task of churning an ocean that would create the wealth that they all valued. The undertaking of churning the milk ocean then can be considered a metaphor for all business organizations, where different people (such as investors, managers, creative professionals, workers) come together to attain the valuable goal of wealth.

As we have mentioned before, according to the Hindu tradition, there is nothing immoral with the pursuit of wealth. Given the fact that the Samudra Manthan story is told in several Puranas, it may not be incorrect to make the inference that the tradition encourages the capitalistic model, where people with different competencies and skills come together to collectively pursue wealth. We can certainly accomplish more together than alone. The story also illustrates many other aspects of the functioning of business organizations. For example, the story shows the importance of people with relevant and complementary traits that the asuras and devas possessed (we will discuss more on this later in the chapter).

Further, the Puranas remind us that it is not enough to select a project that matches the goals but you also need appropriate resources to make the project successful. If you want immortality, you need nectar, for which you have to do the Samudra Manthan, but Samudra Manthan cannot be undertaken without a variety of resources. One also needs appropriate tools to accomplish complex tasks. The churning could not be done without the tools of the Mandara mountain and Vasuki snake. Leaders, workers, collaborative attitude, tools, leadership support, and many more things would be needed to get the project running.

Lastly, the story goes that the devas and asuras had to churn the ocean for eons before the goodies showed up. The challenge during such times is to persist and not give up, at least, until one gets the clear indication that one had chosen a wrong project. But how many times do people and businesses give up on promising projects, just because they were not seeing results within their expected time frame? This does not mean that one should continue to invest in projects that do not give returns. That would be an escalation of commitment into a project with poor prospects (Brockner, 1992; Schmidt & Calantone, 2002; Staw, 1981). What it does mean is that leaders need immense discriminatory power to detect the point where one's healthy persistence is transitioning into the domain of sunk cost (Arkes & Ayton, 1999; Arkes & Blumer, 1985; Friedman et al., 2007). The dhārmic perspective does provide some insights about it, which we discuss later in the chapter.

Managing Profits

The purpose of the Samudra Manthan was to generate outcomes that were valued by the devas and asuras, such as wealth and immortality. And many desirable outcomes indeed came out of the Samudra Manthan process, but needless to say, they were not equally valuable.

When it comes to the wealth goal, the manthan generated two broad categories of outcomes. The first were products such as the Kaustabh jewel, which, as per the legend, is supposed to be the most precious jewel in the entire universe. The second category of outcomes weren't products per se, but representations of power, such as Goddess Lakshmi, who possesses the power to bestow wealth in people's life. The difference between the Kaustabh jewel and Goddess Lakshmi, although they both represent wealth, is that the former is finite but the latter infinite. For somebody with a voracious appetite, even the most expensive prize in the world will eventually run out. We see this happening with some lottery winners (Winkelmann et al., 2011), where the fortune is lost within a few years or decades when it is not managed properly. Thus, having the grace of Goddess Lakshmi, which is the same as gaining the capacity to earn more wealth (artha), is much more valuable. Both at the individual and business level, money becomes more valuable when it is not just used for consumption but also used as an investment for the growth of wealth (Bogliacino & Pianta, 2013; Peng et al., 2007).

Success also enhances our accessibility to pleasure. This is represented by the various Apasaras that came out of the manthan. As we mentioned in the previous chapter, there is nothing morally wrong with enjoying sensual pleasures (kama) as long as one does not get attached to them and does not fail to follow the dharma of performing all duties of life responsibly and competently. Also, as emphasized in the purushārtha theory, it is important to first do one's dharma of developing discipline and working hard—just as the devas and asuras did through the activity of churning the ocean—and only then shift one's attention to pleasure. This idea has overwhelming support in the psychological literature, which shows that the ability to delay gratification is vital to living a happy and successful life (Bembenutty, 2011; Doebel et al., 2020; Mischel, 1974).

Managing Waste

All business ventures have a cost to the environment. From a business ethics and sustainability point of view, this may be one of the most valuable lessons of the churning story. The project of churning the milk ocean not only generated an abundance of valuables but also highly toxic byproducts. Halahal was the toxic waste generated by the churning. This illustrates the fact that business operations will inevitably create waste. The waste needs to be treated with care and disposed of appropriately.

Many people tend to have an implicit assumption that toxic byproducts only come out of industrial organizations or energy companies. But the truth is that all organizations generate waste. Some might think that toxic waste is a characteristic of only some industries—such as the petroleum, coal, automobile, electronics industries—but that would be a wrong interpretation. All enterprises, irrespective of whether it is a small mom-n-pop restaurant or a tax consultant, create waste. Sometimes the waste is a direct byproduct of the production process (e.g., in a nuclear plant). But it may also be the environmental impact of the machines that are being used (e.g., the computers and paper), which is illustrated in the story by the toxic venom leaking out of Vasuki, the snake that was used as the churning rope. Waste has to be handled appropriately, otherwise, it will destroy everything. However, we see in the story that nobody wants to deal with this waste. This continues to be a major problem in modern organizations, where leaders gladly enjoy the benefits of capitalism but are not willing to take any responsibility for the damages that inevitably happen from capitalistic ventures.

The Mindset of Leaders

Most people do not want to deal with these negative aspects of business but the leaders who do, become heroes. Shiva willingly agreed to put himself at risk to deal with the toxic waste of Halahal, and that is the reason, he is worshiped with great reverence by the Hindus. He is the supreme God within the Shaiva tradition of Hinduism.

There is another god in the manthan story who is venerated by the Hindus and that is Vishnu. In the story, we saw that Vishnu willingly took the form of a tortoise (known as the Kurma avatar of Vishnu) to uphold the Mandara Mountain on his back. This highlights the critical importance of people who are willing to take initiative and get their hands dirty when the need arises. The visual imagery of Vishnu supporting the churning task with his tortoise-shaped back also signifies that leaders have to provide all the needed support to the projects that they are involved in; without such support, projects are bound to fail. This lesson also finds extensive support in the leadership literature (Amabile et al., 2004; Bowen, 1998; Horth & Vehar, 2012; Wu & Parker, 2017).

All the characters in the Samudra Manthan story are beings with a significant amount of power. But out of the innumerable asuras and devas in the story, only Vishnu and Shiva are the ones who are still worshipped in the world today. It should also be noted that Vishnu and Shiva were not the official leaders of the gods. Indra, being the king of the gods, was the leader with position power. But it is Vishnu and Shiva who are remembered and worshipped and not Indra because influence happens more through leadership behaviors than through position (Hawkins & Dulewicz, 2009; Leroy et al., 2012). This can also be explained in terms of the differences that are observed between emergent leadership and assigned leadership (Northouse, 2021).

The next important question that needs an answer is, "Why did Goddess Lakshmi choose Vishnu?" The equivalent question in modern-day parlance would be, "What qualities should a leader (or person) have to attract wealth?" In the Puranas, Lakshmi answers this question herself. She says she chose Vishnu because of his abundance mindset. While the asuras and lesser gods started chasing Goddess Lakshmi when she emerged out of the milk ocean, Vishnu did not. Vishnu's name itself reflects his abundance mentality. The verses of the Vishnu Sahasranama—a part of the Mahabharata that literally means 'the thousand names of Vishnu'—start with the names Viswam and Vishnu, both of which emphasize the vastness of his identity. Truly transformative leaders do not ignore the money, but they do not let money drive their thoughts and actions; instead, they have broad visions that aim to benefit the maximum number of people that is possible (Bass, 1990). As per the Puranas, money automatically flows to such leaders.

4.3   THE GUNA THEORY

Beyond Good and Bad

The English translation of the words deva and asura as god and demon, respectively, while common—and we have used it too in this book—is not accurate. The words god and demon give the impression that one is good and the other is evil. Many stories in the tradition show different devas engaging in acts that wouldn't be considered virtuous and the asuras engaging in ones that would be considered highly virtuous. We do share one such story of a virtuous asura, named Bali, in the next chapter.

The collaborative effort of the devas and asuras in the churning of the milk ocean is not a collaboration of the good and evil to accomplish a mutually agreed-upon goal. The concept of good and evil is simplistic. It may be appropriate for young children who are not fully developed to recognize the different shades of gray but is not an accurate representation of the complex world we live in. Even Hollywood movies have moved away from the unidimensional caricature of characters to more complex ones (Cutting, 2015). Most adults would agree that even the best of us have dark sides and the worst of us have bright sides within us. The same argument could also be extended to organizations.

So, is this the difference between devas and asuras, that the devas have more good than bad, and that the asuras have more bad than good? Such explanation is very common across the world, the most famous visual representation of it being the Yin and Yang symbol. This symbol shows a circle divided into two halves by a curved line; one of these halves is colored in black and the other in white; the black half always has a large white dot in it and the white half has a black dot. The symbol has many interpretations but a common one is that there is always some good within evil and evil within good (Fang, 2012; Moeller, 2006). This view of the world is certainly more evolved than the simplistic division of people into good and bad, but it is still an incomplete representation of the world. The Hindu model proposed a three-factor model of worldly reality.

According to the Samkhya school of Hinduism, everything in this world can be divided into two broad categories: *Purusha* (which is the Supreme consciousness that pervades the whole world) and Prakriti (which is the physical and natural world). The Purusha dimension of the world—that people may commonly refer to as God—is so infinite and beyond the limited capacities of our brain that it is impossible to describe in words. Prakriti, which literally means nature, however, is a slightly easier dimension to grapple with. Prakriti includes not just the physical aspects of our being but also the psychological and emotional dimensions.

The concept of Gunas is discussed extensively across all schools of Hinduism but is emphasized heavily within the Samkhya school. The Samkhya school, which also finds an extensive place in the Bhagavad Gita, says that Prakriti consists of three gunas (or qualities), namely sattva, rajas, and tamas. The guna of Rajas refers to a sense of restlessness. It's about being driven. It's about having kinetic energy. The opposite of Rajas would be Tamas, which is often described in terms of inertia, disintegration, lethargy, and ignorance. The third guna is known as Sattva. It is the most ideal form of guna. It is the subtlest state which primarily focuses on truth and awareness. The concept of gunas is completely unique to the Indian philosophies and is an excellent descriptive tool to understand the functioning of the world and the people living in it.

Sattvam laghu prakasakam istam upastam bhakam chalam ca rajah |
Guru varankam eva tamah pradipa vaccharathatho vritih || – Samkhya Kārikā 13.

Sattva is buoyant and illuminating. Rajas is active and exciting. Tamas is heavy and lethargic. They function together for a single purpose like a lamp.

Tamas

Tamas tv ajñāna-jaṁ viddhi mohanaṁ sarva-dehinām |
Pramādālasya-nidrābhis tan nibadhnāti bhārata || – The Bhagavad Gita
(14.8)

Tamas is born of ignorance. It is the cause of illusions. It deludes all living beings through negligence, laziness, and sleep.

Passivity, laziness, and ignorance are the main characteristics of tamas, which refers to the potential energy (static) of things. It is the inertia quality of objects and people, which is characterized in form of a resistance to move unless there is an external force acting on them.

The root word for *tamas* means darkness. People having a predominant tamas guna are also likely to feel more guilt and regret in their lives for not having put their best effort to achieve the things that they desired in their lives.

Tamas may manifest in form of negligence, not caring about anything, and over-indulgence in human beings. A person with excessive tamas may be unwilling to take the initiative necessary for learning, self-improvement, and success. Paradoxically, one may observe high amounts of anger in them, when they attribute their failures in life to the unfairness of the world. From this point of view, tamasic people may be high in External Locus of Control, who tend to blame everybody for their poor life conditions (Baird & Wolak, 2021; Biondo & MacDonald, 1971; Gudjonsson & Singh, 1989).

Rajas

rajo rāgātmakaṁ viddhi tṛishṇā-saṅga-samudbhavam |
tan nibadhnāti kaunteya karma-saṅgena dehinam || – The Bhagavad Gita
(14.7).

Rajas is the quality of passion. It arises from worldly desires and affections, and binds the soul through attachment to utilitarian actions.

The quality of rajas is represented in activity, energy, and passion. That which promotes action or motion is referred to as rajas. Having an excess of rajas may manifest as hyperactivity, inability to rest and sleep, and even overthinking. A classical representation of the rajasic quality may be the Type A Personality, where a person is frantic, active, but also lives a very stressful life (Caplan & Jones, 1975; Ganster et al., 1991).

There is a very desirable aspect about rajasic people because they are passionate and ambitious, and will always achieve more in life than their tamasic counterparts. Rajasic individuals may also seek more stimulation in their environment. This may manifest in several forms, for example, engagement in adventure sports, or regularly traveling to new places, or even frequently engaging in attention-seeking behaviors. However, the negative side of this may manifest in form of greed and disappointments that arise when one is compulsively chasing success.

Sattva

Tatra sattvaṁ nirmalatvāt prakāśhakam anāmayam |
Sukha-saṅgena badhnāti jñāna-saṅgena chānagha || – The Bhagavad Gita (14.6)

Sattva guṇa is the mode of goodness and purity. It illuminates and frees one from engaging in actions that bind us. Sattva binds the soul by creating attachment for a sense of happiness and knowledge.

Sattva guna refers to qualities associated with increased awareness and consciousness. Sattva literally means truth. Thus, the sattva guna means being in tune with the reality of the world. It is not about having fanciful ideas about people—positive or negative. Instead, it is understanding the true nature of everything—positive or negative. A sattvic person may have a deep understanding of the difference between what one really needs and what one wants. In other words, one could say that Viveka—or the ability to correctly discriminate the merits and demerits of various choices—is a key characteristic of the sattva guna.

When people have a predominant sattva guna, they will have greater control over their selves and be happy in their lives. Because they realize the role of blessings in life, they tend to be full of gratitude. Sattva Guna can be seen as a state of balance between being overactive (the rajasic state) and underactive (the tamasic state). Perhaps a more accurate description for the sattva guna would be the ability to intelligently switch between active and passive modes depending on the demands of the situation. Sattva is the quality of being wise, but it is not the passivity that might pervade a philosophical person. Sattva is the quality of being able to act from the state of wisdom that one possesses.

4.4   SATTVA: OPTIMIZING THE THREE GUNAS

The basic idea of the guna theory is that we work towards replacing our Tamas with Rajas, or even better, both our Tamas and Rajas with Sattva. This does not mean that tamas is bad and rajas is good. The Samkhya philosophy specifies that. For example, the quality of tamas would be necessary for us to be able to fall asleep, and it is well established in the medical literature that sleep is one of the critical factors for health (Walker, 2017). However, the sattva quality is always valued because it helps us choose rajas or tamas as per the needs of the situation.

When there is a predominance of the sattva Guna within ourselves and in the organization, there is a lesser need for us to exploit others. And while we still continue to work for the growth of the company (i.e., Rajas), we cease to be exploitative and start adopting more sustainable practices.

The sattva guna is also characterized by an experiential realization of the interconnectedness and unity within the world. And this is illustrated in many slokas. For example, as the Isha Upanishad puts it: "But he who sees everywhere the Self in all existences and all existences in the Self, shrinks not thereafter from aught. He in whom it is the Self-Being that has become all existences that are Becomings, for he has the perfect knowledge, how shall he be deluded, whence shall he have grief who sees everywhere oneness?" (Sri Aurobindo, The Upanishads, Isha Upanishad, v. 6–7, pg. 21).

In other words, if you see the divine in everything, and you see everything in the divine, then life becomes great. This is essentially an approach where you develop a psychological mindset, of interconnectedness with all human beings and all living creatures. When we realize this interconnectedness at a deep experiential level, we then overcome the need to exploit others, to exploit animals, or to exploit the environment.

Sattva allows us to not get into a mindless mode of action. We have earlier emphasized the importance of actions or behaviors in this chapter. However, mindless action or thoughtless actions are likely to more harmful than beneficial to the people and the environment. Thus, from the sattvic perspective, when talking about action, the motive behind the action takes a prominent role in figuring out whether that action is ethical or unethical. Right action is determined based on the right motive. If the motive is free from fear, greed, envy, or any of the other tamasic or rajasic qualities, then the action is considered sattvic.

According to the Hindu perspective, when you do the work out of fear of being reprimanded or out of the greed to acquire more property (i.e., low sattva), you are not necessarily being immoral, but you are not functioning at your best, and such an approach is never sustainable. It is for this reason that intentions matter.

A lot of the current literature on ethics also emphasizes the importance of action in determining what is moral and what is immoral. However, a large part of the ethical literature especially the instrumental rational aspect of ethics focuses on the instrumental usefulness of one's actions in determining whether the action is moral or not. In other words, actions that lead to positive outcomes are considered ethical and actions that do not lead to positive outcomes are considered unethical. This is the instrumental paradigm of ethics.

The problem with such an approach is that this is the approach that has been internalized by businessmen and by economists. What is right is determined only based on the self-interest of how those actions impact the organization in terms of bettering its reputation, lowering its transaction costs, and maximizing its profit. The problem with this paradigm is that it fails to see our interconnectedness with the whole world. In the Hindu tradition, Vishnu became the ruler and the sustainer of the whole universe because his vision and actions encompass the benefit of the entire universe.

Role-Based Ethics

In the Mahabharata, Arjuna faces a moral quandary of whether to fight the battle against the Kauravas. On the one hand, it is his duty or Dharma to fight for justice; it is his duty to work towards the defeat of the evil forces in society. On the other hand, his duty is also to protect his family and to not hurt people whom he loves and respects. In other words, different roads may dictate different dharmic expectations. Now, how do we navigate ourselves through those moral dilemmas where we are pulled in opposite directions, as both the options may seem to be valid?

We see the same happening in business organizations as well, where we feel obligated to maximize profits. But simultaneously, we also feel responsible for the welfare of our employees, for the health of the environment, and the community in which the organization operates. How should a person act or behave when one is pulled in opposite directions? The way Arjuna is confused about Dharma (Bhagavad Gita: 2.7), the same way a CEO may be confused about what the right course of action should be for his organization. Arjuna's mental crisis is in many ways a universal phenomenon. On the one hand, he wants to fulfill his responsibilities as a warrior, but on the other hand, he feels responsible for the lives of his cousins, his teachers, his beloved grandfather. Such conflicts can only be resolved by taking our level of analysis to a higher level. We often get ourselves occupied by the immediate demands that are placed on us, and in the process, we fail to see the larger picture and the role we have to play in this larger picture.

Misplaced Dharma: Do Not Be Dictated by Emotions

When Arjuna is confused about the right course of action, he is essentially worried about the possible consequences of his planned course of action. He becomes sentimental. What may seem like compassion coming from him is not real compassion. It is not true compassion, which we discussed in Chapter 2. We see a similar kind of pressure felt by today's leaders when they attempt to make their organizations overly inclusive. In the process of trying to appease certain groups, they end up making the organization less fair. It is because of the same reason that they are working from their emotions. They let their emotions dictate what is right and what is wrong.

Just because we care for somebody or a group of people does not mean that we should automatically be generous towards them, because it may disrupt the structure of society. For example, helping somebody with money who is an alcoholic or is addicted to drugs out of pity (kripa) will likely harm them more than serving them. Indirectly this will also harm the structure of the society. So, when it comes to ethics, the dharmic perspective is to not get swayed by sentimentality, because when we do that we may end up finding ourselves creating bigger problems than what existed before. It is important to be cognizant of the nature of the person or people whom we are trying to help. The Svabhava or the nature of the person needs to be taken into consideration.

4.5   Strengthening Sattva

The sattvic approach emphasizes proper awareness about the functioning of self and the world, and through this process, reconciles the opposing tendencies authentically and effectively. We have discussed the role of sattva in leadership effectiveness. The question then is how to maximize the sattvic aspect of our personality? There are innumerable techniques within the Hindu tradition to attain this goal. It is beyond the scope of this book to go through them in detail here. However, we briefly enumerate some of these methods below:

Yama and niyama are guidelines proposed in the Patanjali Yoga Sutras (Bryant, 2015) to train the body and mind so that they can withstand the temptations of rajas and tamas, and will have the awareness (sattva) to take decisions that benefit everyone.

The Bhagavad Gita also describes several techniques of enhancing sattva. Karma yoga helps find the balance between the pursuit of goals without having expectations. Raja yoga (or the path of meditation) helps stabilize the restless mind that always tries to rush towards tamasic or rajasic tendencies. A restless mind is a cause of most leadership failures. So for leaders to be effective they should work on conquering their minds through meditation.

As mentioned before, the sattvic approach does not deny the emotional tendencies of the mind; instead, it helps us maximize the benefits of both the rajasic and tamasic tendencies. This is exemplified in Bhakti yoga, where the power of emotions especially those related to love and faith metaphorically move mountains.

Jnana yoga recommends that the leader gains a thorough understanding of the three gunas and their interaction with purusharthas. When leaders have internalized this knowledge, they would be able to work in a way that is authentic and effective.

The Bhāgavata Purana and the Mahabharata provide insights into how an attitude of playfulness (or Leela) that was exemplified by Krishna can enhance sattva. Responsibility and playfulness are seen as opposite ends of the same continuum. In other words, if you have responsibilities, you don't feel playful, and vice versa. However, responsibility and playfulness are independent dimensions. Many leaders (and followers alike) take their work too seriously. However, such seriousness takes a toll on their physical, psychological, and relational health. When we lead life as if it is a play, we aren't too attached to the outcomes. We pursue them but we are not compulsively attached to them. This mindset prevents stress from building up, and paradoxically, leads to greater success for the individual and the organization.

Sattvic Qualities That Strengthen Dharma

According to the Manusmriti (Bühler, 1886), there are ten signs or characteristics indicative of Dharma, that are summarized in the following verse.

> Dhrti Kshama Damah Asteyam Shouchamindriyanigrhah |
> Dhi Vidya Satyamakrodho Dashakam Dharma Lakshanam || (Manusmriti, Verse 6.97)

Using Manu's verse as the foundation, we added a few more qualities based on the aggregation done by Bhaskarananda (1998). These qualities are *Dhriti* is the quality of being courageous and patient in face of challenges. The importance of *dhriti* is explained well in the stoic literature as well, which describes courage as a basic virtue that supports all the other virtues. *Kshama* refers to forgiveness. *Kshama*, however, is not forgiving from a position of weakness, where one might use forgiveness as a ruse for not fighting against injustice.

Dama refers to self-control over one's mind and desires, and the entire system of yoga helps in building this ability. *Asteyam* is the ability to withstand temptations and not engage in stealing. *Shaucha* refers to cleanliness and purity, both internal and external. This is the opposite of tamas, where people stop taking care of their bodies, clothes, and surroundings. At a psychological level, it means regularly cleaning up unresolved negative emotions, desires, and attachments from the mind.

Indriya nigraha is the equivalent of *dama* for the physical body. While *dama* is focused on gaining control over the mind, *indriya nigraha* focuses on controlling our sense organs, they are the first gate from which we slip into compulsive rajas and tamas. *Dhī* refers to wisdom, the guidance of calm reason, the power to discriminate between right and wrong, analysis, and identification of the proper path toward the benefit of all beings, irrespective of difficulties and temptations. Another word for *Dhī* that is commonly used in the Hindu literature is *Viveka*. *Vidya* is the internalized spiritual and practical knowledge that helps us be effective in the world. And *Satyam* is the commitment to truth or sattva. It means to not operate in the world from a state of delusion. *Akrodha* refers to control over the specific emotion of anger, because of its immense power. It does not mean that one should never be angry because anger can be used for constructive purposes. For example, Gandhi experienced extreme anger when he was pushed out of the train in South Africa for not being white, but he nurtured that anger in a way that reduced its negative aspects while providing him with the energy to fight injustice. *Shanti* refers to peace, *Santosha* refers to contentment, and *Tyāga* to renunciation of self-ishness. These are desirable mental states but are rarely achieved when in the grips of rajas or tamas. *Daya* is compassion, the quality that we have discussed in detail in Chapter 2. *Hrī* refers to modesty and humility. Although humility wasn't considered an important factor for leadership effectiveness, modern research on the topic has confirmed its importance in leadership effectiveness. On the flip side, hubris, which is the lack of *Hrī*, is one of the most common causes of leadership derailment.

4.6 CONCLUSION

Over the past couple of decades, leadership scholars have placed a considerable emphasis on moral (Avolio & Gardner, 2005; Brown & Treviño, 2006; Lemoine et al., 2019) and spiritual (Ashar & Lane-Maher, 2004; Benefiel et al., 2014; Schutte, 2016) aspects of leadership. This is a significant shift of focus in the leadership literature (Lemoine et al., 2019). Although it may be difficult to pinpoint the exact cause of this shift, the many high profile corporate scandals that plagued the late 1990s and early 2000s (Ghoshal, 2005), and the corresponding drop in trust in leaders (Hurley, 2006; Montoya et al., 2007) certainly played a role. Unfortunately, compared to other professionals, business leaders continue to be rated the lowest on honesty and ethical standards (Gallup Inc, 2018).

People are also increasingly concerned about the damage that the unfettered growth of large corporations has caused to individuals, families, societies, and the environment (Mishra & Schmidt, 2018). While it is encouraging to see a shift in the literature towards more moral and spiritual viewpoints of leadership, we still have a long way to go before we see actual changes in the orientation of leaders. This is expected because changing mindsets and behavioral patterns of individuals, including those of leaders, take time. However, this is also an opportunity for us to critically evaluate our current models of moral and spiritual leadership to make sure that they are valid and useful to leaders of business organizations.

REFERENCES

Amabile, T. M., Schatzel, E. A., Moneta, G. B., & Kramer, S. J. (2004). Leader behaviors and the work environment for creativity: Perceived leader support. *The Leadership Quarterly, 15*(1), 5–32.

Arkes, H. R., & Ayton, P. (1999). The sunk cost and Concorde effects: Are humans less rational than lower animals? *Psychological Bulletin, 125*(5), 591.

Arkes, H. R., & Blumer, C. (1985). The psychology of sunk cost. *Organizational Behavior and Human Decision Processes, 35*(1), 124–140.

Ashar, H., & Lane-Maher, M. (2004). Success and spirituality in the new business paradigm. *Journal of Management Inquiry, 13*(3), 249–260.

Avolio, B. J., & Gardner, W. L. (2005). Authentic leadership development: Getting to the root of positive forms of leadership. *The Leadership Quarterly, 16*(3), 315–338.

Baird, V., & Wolak, J. (2021). Why some blame politics for their personal problems. *American Politics Research*, 1532673X211013463.

Bass, B. M. (1990). From transactional to transformational leadership: Learning to share the vision. *Organizational Dynamics, 18*(3), 19–31.

Bembenutty, H. (2011). Academic delay of gratification and academic achievement. In H. Bembunutty (Ed.), *Self regulated learning: New direction for teaching and learning.* Wiley Periodicals, Inc.

Benefiel, M., Fry, L. W., & Geigle, D. (2014). Spirituality and religion in the workplace: History, theory, and research. *Psychology of Religion and Spirituality, 6*(3), 175.

Bhaskarananda, S. (1998). *The essentials of Hinduism.* Sri Ramakrishna Math Printing Press.

Biondo, J., & MacDonald, A., Jr. (1971). Internal-external locus of control and response to influence attempts 1. *Journal of Personality, 39*(3), 407–419.

Bogliacino, F., & Pianta, M. (2013). Innovation and demand in industry dynamics: R&D, new products and profits. In *Long term economic development* (pp. 95–112). Springer.

Bowen, G. L. (1998). Effects of leader support in the work unit on the relationship between work spillover and family adaptation. *Journal of Family and Economic Issues, 19*(1), 25–52.

Brockner, J. (1992). The escalation of commitment to a failing course of action: Toward theoretical progress. *Academy of Management Review, 17*(1), 39–61.

Brown, M. E., & Treviño, L. K. (2006). Ethical leadership: A review and future directions. *The Leadership Quarterly, 17*(6), 595–616.

Bryant, E. F. (2015). *The yoga sutras of Patanjali: A new edition, translation, and commentary.* North Point Press.

Bühler, G. (1886). *The laws of Manu* (Vol. 25). Clarendon Press.

Caplan, R. D., & Jones, K. W. (1975). Effects of work load, role ambiguity, and Type A personality on anxiety, depression, and heart rate. *Journal of Applied Psychology, 60*(6), 713.

Cutting, J. E. (2015). The framing of characters in popular movies. *Art & Perception, 3*(2), 191–212.

Doebel, S., Michaelson, L. E., & Munakata, Y. (2020). Good things come to those who wait: Delaying gratification likely does matter for later achievement (a commentary on Watts, Duncan, & Quan, 2018). *Psychological Science, 31*(1), 97–99.

Fang, T. (2012). Yin Yang: A new perspective on culture. *Management and Organization Review, 8*(1), 25–50.

Friedman, D., Pommerenke, K., Lukose, R., Milam, G., & Huberman, B. A. (2007). Searching for the sunk cost fallacy. *Experimental Economics, 10*(1), 79–104.

Gallup Inc. (2018). *Honesty/ethics in professions*. https://news.gallup.com/poll/1654/Honesty-Ethics-Professions.aspx

Ganster, D. C., Schaubroeck, J., Sime, W. E., & Mayes, B. T. (1991). The nomological validity of the Type A personality among employed adults. *Journal of Applied Psychology, 76*(1), 143.

Ghoshal, S. (2005). Bad management theories are destroying good management practices. *Academy of Management Learning & Education, 4*(1), 75–91.

Gudjonsson, G. H., & Singh, K. K. (1989). The revised Gudjonsson blame attribution inventory. *Personality and Individual Differences, 10*(1), 67–70.

Hawkins, J., & Dulewicz, V. (2009). Relationships between leadership style, the degree of change experienced, performance and follower commitment in policing. *Journal of Change Management, 9*(3), 251–270.

Horth, D. M., & Vehar, J. (2012). *Becoming a leader who fosters innovation*. Center for Creative Leadership.

Hurley, R. F. (2006). The decision to trust. *Harvard Business Review, 84*(9), 55–62.

Lemoine, G. J., Hartnell, C. A., & Leroy, H. (2019). Taking stock of moral approaches to leadership: An integrative review of ethical, authentic, and servant leadership. *Academy of Management Annals*(ja).

Leroy, H., Palanski, M. E., & Simons, T. (2012). Authentic leadership and behavioral integrity as drivers of follower commitment and performance. *Journal of Business Ethics, 107*(3), 255–264.

Mischel, W. (1974). Processes in delay of gratification. In *Advances in experimental social psychology* (Vol. 7, pp. 249–292). Elsevier.

Mishra, P., & Schmidt, G. B. (2018). How can leaders of multinational organizations be ethical by contributing to corporate social responsibility initiatives? Guidelines and pitfalls for leaders trying to do good. *Business Horizons, 61*(6), 833–843.

Moeller, H.-G. (2006). *The philosophy of the Daodejing*. Columbia University Press.

Montoya, R. M., Purvin, D. M., Pittinsky, T. L., & Rosenthal, S. A. (2007). National Leadership Index 2007: A national study of confidence in leadership.

Northouse, P. G. (2021). *Leadership: Theory and practice*. Sage.

Peng, T.-C.M., Bartholomae, S., Fox, J. J., & Cravener, G. (2007). The impact of personal finance education delivered in high school and college courses. *Journal of Family and Economic Issues, 28*(2), 265–284.

Schmidt, J. B., & Calantone, R. J. (2002). Escalation of commitment during new product development. *Journal of the Academy of Marketing Science, 30*(2), 103–118.

Schutte, P. J. (2016). Workplace spirituality: A tool or a trend? *HTS Theological Studies, 72*(4), 1–5.

Staw, B. M. (1981). The escalation of commitment to a course of action. *Academy of Management Review, 6*(4), 577–587.

Walker, M. (2017). *Why we sleep: Unlocking the power of sleep and dreams*. Simon & Schuster.

Winkelmann, R., Oswald, A. J., & Powdthavee, N. (2011). *What happens to people after winning the lottery*. Paper presented at the European Economic Association & Econometric Society Parallel Meetings.

Wu, C.-H., & Parker, S. K. (2017). The role of leader support in facilitating proactive work behavior: A perspective from attachment theory. *Journal of Management, 43*(4), 1025–1049.

CHAPTER 5

Organizational Dharma

5.1 Charity with Pride

A long time ago, there lived an Asura (demon) king named Mahābali. At the time of the Samudra Manthan (described in Chapter 3), he had temporarily possessed the Amrita (nectar for eternal life) as well that made him immortal. Although a demon, he was also the descendant of dharmic stalwarts such as Prahlāda and sage Kashyapa. Like his ancestor, Prahlāda, he was a great devotee of Vishnu. So, he had a lot of goodness in him. He was known to be extremely benevolent and generous. Everyone was happy in his kingdom because he gave generously to everyone who came to him for help. He was the epitome of the Marxist maxim, "to each according to his need."

One morning, Lord Vishnu came to meet him disguised as a young dwarf Brahmin (the Vāmana Avatār). When Mahābali asked Him to express His wish, Vishnu simply replied that He wanted land equivalent to the area that He could cover in three steps. Mahābali laughed at the smallness of the little Brahmin's thinking because he took pride in fulfilling the biggest wishes of people. But Vishnu insisted that he did not want anything more and would be content with 3-steps' worth of land. Mahābali pledged to fulfill the little Brahmin's wish.

But the moment Mahābali made that commitment, Vishnu metamorphosed into a giant of infinite proportions. He took all of Swarga (heaven)

P. Mishra and S. Kalagnanam, *Managing by Dharma*, Palgrave Studies in Workplace Spirituality and Fulfillment, https://doi.org/10.1007/978-3-030-90669-6_5

in His first step and the entire Earth with His second. With no space left for His third step, Vishnu asked where He should place His third step. The great-hearted Mahābali offered his head. Vishnu took that step, which pushed Mahābali into pātāla (netherworld).

The legend has it that Lord Vishnu was pleased with Mahābali's commitment. So, He granted Mahābali a boon that permitted him to come to Earth's surface once every year. The day the metaphoric Mahābali comes back to Earth is associated with bountiful harvest and is celebrated as Onam, one of the largest festivals in the Indian state of Kerala.

King Mahābali was extremely good-natured and charitable. So why did God push him into the netherworld? According to some communist scholars, Mahābali's story is a representation of Brahmins' trickery and oppression of the lower caste and Adivasi (or tribal) people (Devika, 2010; Kalidasan, 2016). Anyone who is even cursorily familiar with the ancient Hindu literature will laugh at the absurdity of such interpretations because there are innumerable stories of Gods punishing Brahmins when they performed bad karma (the most notable example here would be that of Lord Rāma killing Rāvana who was a Brahmin) and rewarding people from the lower strata of the society when they performed good karma (e.g., Lord Rāma's blessing an old tribal lady named, Shabari). Since the focus of our book is not to critique anti-Hindu literature, we will not delve any deeper into this discussion, and instead, provide our interpretation of Mahābali's story.

Unchecked charity is not sustainable and often creates more problems than it solves. This is illustrated again and again in the Hindu literature through many other stories. Another notable story is that of Karna, a warrior in the Mahabharata, who was reverentially addressed as Dānavira Karna (or the most charitable and fearless, Karna). The extent of his charity was such that he even gave away his Kawatch—the divine armor that made him invincible—during the Mahabharata war, which ultimately led to his death. While dying, he complains to Lord Krishna about the unfairness with which he was killed, but who is really to be blamed if you are so blinded by your identity of being a charitable person that you willingly and voluntarily give away the armor that would have protected you on the battlefield?

In Mahābali's case, when Vishnu in the form of Vāmana avatar requested for three paces of land, Mahābali's guru, the learned Shukrācharya who could foresee the future, beseeched him to not agree to the Vāmana's request, but Mahābali was so enamored by his grandiose vision "that all of life's problems will be solved by distributing wealth," (Pattanaik, 2013) that he simply sneered at him.

Mahabāli's story also illustrates the limits of charity. Charity can never satiate the "hunger" of human beings because human beings' hunger for more (i.e., greed) is unlimited, but the world's resources are limited.

5.2 WHAT IS ORGANIZATIONAL DHARMA?

An organization is a collective of individuals and, in its own right, can be labeled as a 'living' entity. Therefore, it is natural to consider how a set of principles that enables individuals to prosper in a disciplined or responsible manner can be applied to organizations (Parel, 2006). Moreover,

> since businesses today operate in an environment characterized by increasing levels of competitive and regulatory forces, they are also accountable to a broader set of stakeholders than before. Businesses are required to make significant trade-offs when making decisions. This is particularly important in large organizations where (1) decision making is generally dispersed across several hierarchical levels, (2) there is greater possibility of the organization being structured along functional lines, (3) there may be practical difficulties with respect to direct supervision and/or oversight and (4) there is greater possibility of diversity among employees in terms of age, experience, expectations, and belief systems. (Kalagnanam et al., 2016)

The issue of direct supervision and/or oversight is critical in the current context of COVID where many organizations have transitioned at least partially to a remote environment. A potential challenge associated with the lack of direct supervision or oversight, combined with the presence of multiple decision-makers at different levels within an organization, is the presence of egoistic individuals like Mahābali whose self-pride may be more important than the organization's priorities.

According to Bhaskarananda (1998), there are five levels of dharma—individual, family, society, nation, and humankind (see Fig. 5.1). The idea of individual-level dharma is that it helps individuals live their life responsibly by adhering to values and principles as well as understanding their duties or responsibilities towards the remaining four levels. Similarly, dharma as a regulative principle at especially the remaining four

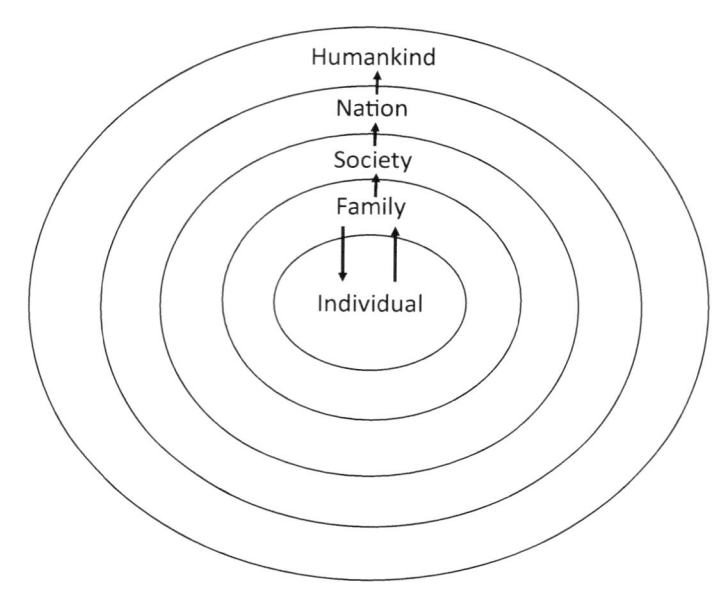

Fig. 5.1   Dharma levels (individual) (Adapted from Bhaskarananda [1998])

levels—family, society, nation, and humankind—helps bind a family or a society. This is important because it is not uncommon for societies (or civilizations) to become extinct.

Within a managerial context, Hawley introduced the term organizational dharma to explicitly recognize the fact that every organization, as a collective of individuals, must adhere to a set of principles which make up its inner law (Hawley, 1993, 1995).

> There is a collective *dharma*, an organizational inner law – and each organization has its own. The traits of courage, self-discipline, goodness and doing right (emphasis on *right*, remember) are the marks of collective character just as they are of individual character. Each organization must also follow its own collective heart and soul, or pay the price. (Hawley, 1995)

Our research suggests that most organizations believe in the importance of organizational-level dharma, although individual organizations may conceptualize it in their own unique ways. Examples of the different conceptualizations include 'being true to the purpose or the organization's reason for existence', 'code of conduct', 'set of things that are allowed/not allowed or recommended/not recommended', 'organizational common sense', 'sacred mantra', 'organizational values', 'organizing towards a way of working towards a common goal', 'moral commitment', 'source of the big piece of the organization', 'set of principles', 'duty', and 'culture'. The idea of a sacred mantra or a list of things allowed or not allowed speaks to the non-negotiables that every organization must clearly articulate. Concerning duty, it is important to understand that employees have duties towards their internal and external stakeholders. Likewise, the organization also has duties towards its internal and external stakeholders (see Fig. 5.2). More important, however, is to know who the stakeholders are and what are the obligations of the organization and each individual employee towards these stakeholder groups.

The idea underlying the development of an organizational-level common sense is that individuals within an organization may vary in terms

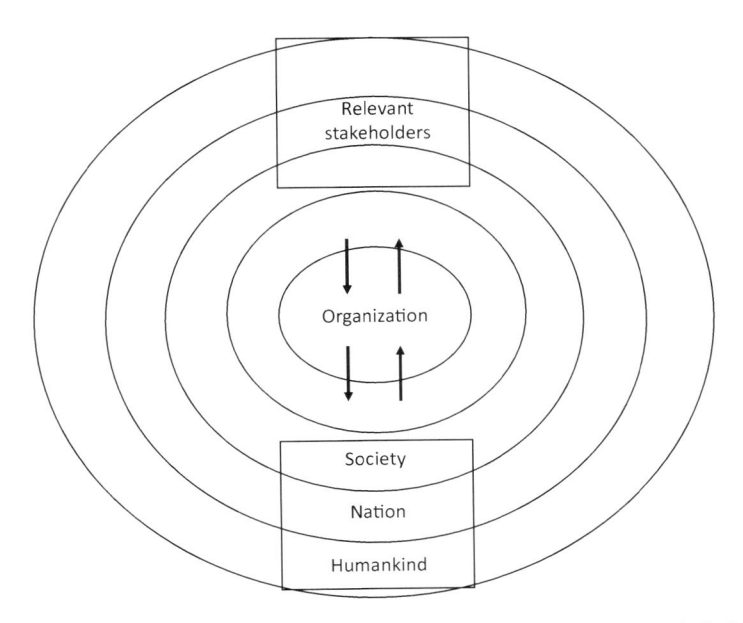

Fig. 5.2 Dharma levels (organization) (Adapted form Bhaskarananda [1998])

of how they conceptualize and practice dharma. In other words, it may be perceived as translating philosophical dharma into practical dharma. Organizational common sense is designed to arrive at an average level of dharma that appeals to everyone; however, senior leadership has the responsibility of continuously moving the average up while also reducing the variabilities that may exist across individuals. As such the leader of the organization plays a critical role in shaping the organization's dharma or the core set of principles.

Regardless of how different organizations conceptualize dharma, the general consensus is that it is important to articulate it while at the same time recognizing that it is not always easy to do that. Managing by dharma is about "… bringing that truth with you when you go to work every day. It's the fusing of spirit, character, human values, and decency in the workplace and in life as a whole" (Hawley, 1993, p. 1).

5.3   Purpose of Organizational Dharma

The very purpose of dharma is to keep everything together, and the purpose of organizational dharma is to sustain or keep the organization together. This is possible by conceptualizing organizational dharma in three mutually reinforcing ways: as a goal, as a foundation, and as actions/decisions (see Fig. 5.3). The purpose of conceptualizing it as a goal is learning. It is common knowledge that organizations experience change in the form of people, processes, technology, opportunities,

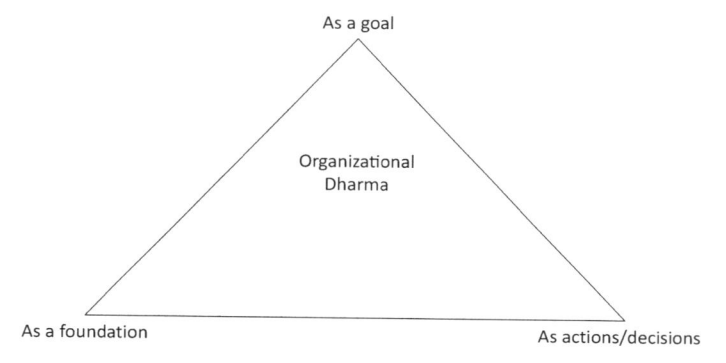

Fig. 5.3   Dharma triangle

regulations, and other factors. Therefore, regular reinforcement of the principles helps employees understand them within the context of changes taking place. As such knowledge/learning is an important quality underlying dharma; therefore, continuous learning or continuous improvement (Kaizen) of knowledge regarding values, policies, procedures, techniques, stakeholders, contextual environment, market, regulations, and other important factors is critical. The purpose of conceptualizing as a foundation is to understand that the set of values and/or principles that underlie dharma forms the basis for decision-making and, more importantly, helps guide the organization in conflict situations. The actions/decisions provide a basis for assessing how well individuals have internalized the organizational dharma and are able to apply them in their day-to-day activities, regardless of whether they are strategic or operational in nature. Taken together the dharma triangle in Fig. 5.3 provides the basis for an entity to function as a responsible organization.

The term 'responsibility', in the context of a business, is used in a variety of ways—(1) responsibilities towards its primary and secondary stakeholders such as employees, customers, suppliers, owners, law, government, society, planet (see Fig. 5.2), (2) ethical or moral responsibilities, and (3) managerial responsibilities. In other words, responsibility is an important word in the vocabulary of a modern corporation. This point is further reinforced by other scholars. Carroll (1990) emphasizes the importance of making decisions keeping in mind those who will be affected by the decision. Fombrun and Foss (2004) suggest that corporate ethics is now considered as being central both as a set of principles and in decision-making, which represent two of the three vertices of the dharma triangle presented in Fig. 5.3.

However, simply using the word in corporate publications is different from acting responsibly. For instance, a quick scan of the value statements of the five largest Canadian banks reveals terms such as accountability, diversity, empathy, integrity, passion, respect, responsibility, and trust. Yet, a recently released report by the Canadian Broadcasting Corporation (CBC) documents the stories of employees from all the big banks "… of how they feel pressured to upsell, trick and even lie to customers to meet unrealistic targets and keep their jobs" (Johnson, 2017), and this resulted in many individuals quitting their jobs. This example potentially reinforces the observation made by Pava (2003) who states as follows:

"Organizations demand more time, psychic energy, loyalty, and imagination from employees than ever before, but continue to treat them as if they were interchangeable parts" (p. 393).

Another report by CBC News states as follows:

> The Canada Revenue Agency offered amnesty to multi-millionaire clients caught using what's been called an offshore tax "sham" on the Isle of Man — a reprieve that was supposed to remain secret and out of the public eye until it was uncovered by a CBC News/Radio-Canada investigation. The amnesty allows for "high net worth" clients of the accounting giant KPMG to be free from any future civil or criminal prosecution — as well as any penalties or fines — for their involvement in the controversial scheme.... It promised KPMG clients that the CRA would not impose any penalties for taxes dodged in a scheme that lasted more than a decade. (Cashore et al., 2016)

As a final example, the State of Tax Justice 2020 "... reports that the world is losing over \$427 billion (USD) in a tax year to international tax abuse" (Tax Justice Network, 2020). The loss in the European region alone is over \$184 billion which is equivalent to the annual salaries of over 4.6 million nurses in the region and over 17.5% of the region's combined spending on education (Tax Justice Network, 2020).

These examples speak of the lack of responsibility displayed by large corporations, government, wealthy individuals, and managers and reinforce the importance of understanding and internalizing the concept of responsibility and acting responsibly. We believe this can only be possible if organizations understand dharma and furthermore adopt it as an underlying philosophy to guide decision-making at all levels within the organization.

A responsible organization, through adopting responsibility as its core philosophy, will not only align with what Reidenbach and Robin (1991) call an ethical organization, Duerr (2004) terms as a contemplative organization, and Danak (2010) calls a divine enterprise, but actually help organizations advance towards being truly ethical, contemplative, or divine. What does it mean to say adopting responsibility as its core philosophy? Simply stated, this means putting the concept of responsibility 'front and center' at all times.

The Oxford Dictionary (Hawkins, 1988) defines responsibility as being responsible; it further offers multiple meanings for the word responsible, such as: (1) legally or morally obliged to carry out a duty, (2) having to account for one's actions (accountability), (3) capable of rational conduct, and (4) trustworthy. Therefore, a responsible organization, by definition, should be trustworthy, conduct itself in a rational manner within the bounds of legality *and* morality, and be accountable to all its stakeholders (Carroll, 1991; Pava & Krausz, 2006; Reidenbach & Robin, 1991; Sivakumar, 2008). Deshpandé and Raina (2011) document one of the most unprecedented displays of responsible behavior by the Taj Group of Hotels, specifically the hotel located in Mumbai, when it became the target of a terrorist attack in November 2008.

> During the onslaught on the Taj Mumbai, 31 people died and 28 were hurt, but the hotel received only praise the day after. Its guests were overwhelmed by employees' dedication to duty, their desire to protect guests without regard to personal safety, and their quick thinking. Restaurant and banquet staff rushed people to safe locations such as kitchens and basements. Telephone operators stayed at their posts, alerting guests to lock doors and not step out. Kitchen staff formed human shields to protect guests during evacuation attempts. As many as 11 Taj Mumbai employees—a third of the hotel's casualties—laid down their lives while helping between 1,200 and 1,500 guests escape. (Deshpandé & Raina, 2011)

Media reports following the attack document the commitment of the Tata Group (Taj is part of the Tata Group) towards the families of employees who lost their lives and "… a large number of people who had nothing to do with the Tatas … [including] railway employees, police staff and pedestrians" (Devnani, 2009).

According to Pruzan (2008),

> … a growing number of sensitive corporate leaders (as well as thoughtful leadership theoreticians) have obtained the insight that ethical and responsible business behaviour is vital for an organization's success in a broad, inclusive service-oriented interpretation of that word. Profits are understood by such leaders less as *the* [emphasis original] goal and more as a necessary means that can enable the organization to achieve its many goals, such as, to be a wonderful place to work with proud and happy employees; to develop, produce and market products and services of highest quality; to deliver a satisfactory return to the owners and to be respected as a good 'corporate citizen' (p. 104).

By extension, the definition of a responsible organization applies to every employee, particularly for individuals in positions of managerial authority and responsibility. Hawley (1995) notes that "[t]here is a particular *dharma* for managers ... because they are a seat of responsibility." This point about a manager's responsibility is further echoed by Teal (1996) as follows:

> In one form or another, managing has become one of the world's most common jobs, and yet we make demands on managers that are nearly impossible to meet. For starters, we ask them to acquire a long list of more or less traditional management skills in ... [many] areas. We also demand that they master the management arts – strategy, persuasion, negotiation, writing, speaking, listening. In addition, we ask them to assume responsibility for organizational success, make a great deal of money and share it generously. We also require them to demonstrate the qualities that define leadership, integrity, and character – things like vision, fortitude, passion, sensitivity, commitment, insight, intelligence, ethical standards, charisma, luck, courage, tenacity, even from time to time, humility. Finally, we insist that they should be our friends, mentors or guardians, perpetually alert to our best interests. Practicing this common profession *adequately* [emphasis original], in other words, requires people to display on an everyday basis the combined skills of St. Peter, Peter the Great, and the Great Houdini....
>
> One reason for the scarcity of managerial greatness is that in educating and training managers, we focus too much on technical proficiency and too little on character. The management sciences ... are things we can almost take for granted these days. But we're still in the Dark Ages when it comes to teaching people how to *behave* [emphasis original] like great managers – somehow instilling in them capacities such as courage and integrity that can't be taught. Perhaps as a consequence, we've developed a tendency to downplay the importance of the human element in managing.

5.4   Qualities Underlying Dharma

According to Noss (2003), a person "... who follows *Dharma* is faithful in the performance of prescribed duties ... for the sake of the smooth working of the divinely ordained society" (p. 109). As explained in Chapter 4, there are many qualities of a dharmic individual (Bühler & Müller, 1969, 1886; Bhaskarananda, 1998). It is important to recognize that these qualities are not limited to a single religion or faith group. For instance, the quality of *dayā*—kindness/compassion—is mentioned in Biblical verses as compassion and kindness (Colossians 3:12), in Confucianism as love, benevolence, and humaneness, and in the First Nations principles as love. Similarly, the quality of *satyam*—truth—is mentioned as truth in the First Nations Principles and Biblical verses (Psalm 15: 2–5 and John 3:21), and as honesty and trustworthiness in Confucianism.

Do these qualities apply at an organizational level and in what ways can they manifest themselves within an organization? One cannot deny the importance of *satyam* (truth), *vidya* (knowledge/learning), and *asteyam* (non-covetousness) as relevant qualities that an organization must possess. However, qualities like *dayā* (kindness, compassion), *indriya nigraha* (discipline of the body, mind, and senses), *akrodha* (absence of anger), and especially *hrī* (modesty) and *santosha* (contentment) are not normally associated with organizations, especially businesses. This is because businesses have traditionally focused on maximizing profits and shareholder value (Friedman, 1970), and employees are considered as simply a factor of production to achieve its profitability goals. Our research revealed to us that only two qualities among 15 included in the list were not deemed relevant or transferrable to an organizational context—*indriya nigraha* and *santosha*. The remaining 13 qualities were endorsed by between 26% and 52% of the individuals we asked, and the top five among these 13 are *akrodha* (absence of anger), *dayā* (kindness/compassion), *vidya* (knowledge/learning), *dhriti* (determination/firmness), and *satyam* (truth). The recognition of the importance of qualities like 'absence of anger' and 'kindness/compassion' by close to half of our interviewees is indeed very encouraging. A key question, however, is 'How can these qualities be manifested and sustained within an organization'?

It is widely accepted that a business can be considered as being successful when it serves multiple stakeholders, which means "… creating healthy returns for shareholders, … emphasizing good jobs for employees, a clean environment, responsible relations with community and reliable products for consumers" (Sivakumar, 2008, p. 353). Numerous examples, enumerated below, illustrate how different qualities manifest themselves within an organization.

Excel Industries Limited's 60th annual report lists compassion as a key quality that underlies its commitment towards the 'greater good' (https://excelind.co.in/downloads/annual-reports/60th%20Annual%20Report%202020-21.pdf):

> To balance the needs of others with our growth, it is essential that we first understand their concerns. From the senior management to the workers on the factory floor, everyone at the Excel Family is committed to making a difference to our larger goals, and it all begins with a sympathetic ear and an open mind.

The former Chief Executive Officer (CEO) of an auto parts supplier emphasized the importance of extending kindness/compassion beyond the company's employee base to those of outsourced service providers such as housekeeping, security, and cafeteria personnel. Strictly speaking, the company does not have to worry about what happens to the service providers and their employees, but its firm stand is that these personnel will also be treated with the same level of dignity and respect that the company's direct employees experience.

Employees are perhaps the most important stakeholder for any organization; therefore, extending kindness/compassion towards employees is equally important. For instance, Patagonia celebrates every aspect of its employees through the holistic value that it places on them (Henneman, 2011). Similarly, Jamshedji Nusserwanji Tata, founder of the Tata Group of Companies, recognized the importance of employees and practiced compassion through providing several benefits to employees and their families (Sivakumar, 2008). Being kind and compassionate towards employees or other stakeholders does not mean ignoring incompetence, lack of commitment, or tardiness. This is where it becomes important to separate the individual from the activity/event/task to ensure that criticism is targeted not towards the individual but towards the activity/event/task, and appropriate corrective action taken. As explained by a senior executive of a large firm, compassion towards an incompetent employee can be expressed in the form of delaying the firing an employee by two days (Monday instead of the previous Friday) so that the employee gets paid for an additional two days.

Two other qualities that closely relate to kindness/compassion are absence of anger and forgiveness. The CEO of a mid-sized company observed that it is natural to get angry or upset in certain situations regardless of whether they pertain to actions (effort), results, or situations especially in the context of meetings. However, he also recognized that it is important to practice absence of anger at that moment to deal with the situation and get down to solution mode after the meeting. A common consequence of not practicing absence of anger is that it can easily create fear among employees, as illustrated by a former senior executive of a large global organization.

> One of the companies I have worked in, the Head Honcho was given to short temper. He had a very serious anger management problem. On some trivial thing, he would lose it. In fact, in one of the town hall meetings, somebody asked a question, which he thought was irrelevant or stupid or motivated to project the organization in a bad way. Something went wrong, didn't click, so he really fired him and that was the early question in the town hall second, or third, or fourth question. He really fired him in front of hundreds of people and after that no more questions, right, everybody withdrew into their shell and then he abruptly ended the town hall because no questions were coming. Later, he felt very bad about it, and we shelved the Friday management meeting, it had all the senior people, heads of department, we used to meet with him, and he asked us a day later 'on that day, I should not [have been so angry], and we all said yeah, you messed up bad, big time, in front of us. He asked his secretary to get that [person who was fired] into the board room if he was free; he was called and he came really nervous, really afraid. Then he [the executive] apologized to him in front of all of us, we were his [direct reports], all heads of departments and he said 'look I am very sorry, I should not have done that. Actually, I would have loved to call the entire town hall again but that would mean calling people from different parts of [the city] into one building and that would be too much of a waste of time for everybody, but I apologize to you'. So, it was very bad; he lost a bit of his – what should I say – esteem thing, because of his anger. So, anger particularly when you are in a higher position, for whatever [reason] is bad.

According to the Greater Good Magazine, forgiveness is a conscious decision on the part of one individual (or group) to "release feelings of resentment … toward a person or group who has harmed you …." (https://greatergood.berkeley.edu/topic/forgiveness/definition). However, it is important to note that forgiveness is not about condoning undesirable actions or excusing offenses, especially in an organizational context. Our research suggests that many organizations practice forgiveness by not penalizing an employee or supplier for their first mistake or poor decision. Instead, they see it as an opportunity to coach the individual or the group so that such mistakes can be avoided in the future. The key question in such situations is how many times should the same individual or group be forgiven for their actions because of the implications of their actions on the organization. The following example illustrates this potential tension (paraphrased to maintain the flow of the discussion).

> The college that I am involved with as a volunteer Board member is run by some very, very nice people, too nice actually. Some are engineers by qualification, but they all are very philanthropically oriented. They would not harm an ant, but they don't have an articulated set of values and they don't act on non-performers. I think they know their duty, look, they are smart enough to know that they have to do these things. Somehow, they are reluctant to, maybe they are too soft or, I am not really sure as to why, why they are not. Maybe, you know, it's a toss between two goods. For example, they will not take bribes to admit a student, they will not take bribes from a student, give it to the university, and make him or her pass. That they will not do. But, in say a situation where a lecturer or a staff member is doing something wrong, he is stealing money from the college or remaining absent, not coming to class on time, forgiving such an individual repeatedly is in a way doing good to him, not cutting his increment, or not firing him, helping him and his family to sustain their livelihood, right? But you are hurting your institution. You are setting a bad example for others. So, here in a way by condoning that person repeatedly, you are doing a good thing to him as a human being, but you are hurting the organization, you are not doing justice towards the other greater good.

Organizational peace of mind, as a quality, is important so that employees and other stakeholders can discharge their roles and engage with the company in a calm manner. Accidents and other unpleasant activities or incidents are never desirable, but they do happen every such occurrence can disturb an organization's peace of mind. As an example, consider the situation where a shopfloor employee loses a portion of his hand due to an accident; this is disruptive not just for other shopfloor employees but also for management. Another example, particularly relevant in the context of COVID, is temporary or permanent layoffs. Restoring the organization's peace of mind becomes priority number one to ensure that employees regain their faith in the company and maintain their sense of belongingness.

Another quality, closely linked to peace of mind, is truth. Our field research suggests that many senior executives consider truth as a core value—a non-negotiable quality—that can lay the foundation for an organization's character and attach significant importance to it. A strong commitment to truth creates the path for an organization to be honest, and this enables the organization to practice transparency, remain fearless, and maintain its integrity.

The Oxford Dictionary (Hawkins, 1988) defines the term transparent as: (1) allowing light to pass through so that objects behind can be seen clearly, (2) easily understood; (of an excuse or motive etc.) of such a kind that the truth behind it is easily perceived, and (3) clear and unmistakable. Each of the three definitions is relevant to the functioning of a dharmic organization and all three speak to the notion of clarity in developing, communicating, and applying decision criteria and ultimately clarity in communicating the processes and outcomes. Another aspect of transparency is that the same information should be available to all stakeholders. Pava and Krausz (2006) highlight the importance of transparency but caution that "... not all stakeholders have a legitimate right to all corporate information." We add to their observation by saying that not all stakeholders may have an equal interest in all the information. However, we argue that a truly dharmic organization should have nothing to hide and should be willing to make information available to *all* stakeholders when asked. Clearly, we are talking about information beyond the legally required disclosures. This is not easy for an organization to accept and adopt but think about the credibility of the organization among stakeholders and the respect it is likely to command from exhibiting such a high level of transparency!

Klassen et al. (2019) highlight the practice of truth by a large nongovernmental organization (NGO) with a presence across India. Essentially, truthfulness and transparency allow this NGO to be accountable to its two main stakeholder groups, funding agencies, and beneficiaries of the services that it provides.

> In keeping with the values of honesty and transparency, under-expenditures are either returned or explicit permission is obtained for spending on different projects. Similarly, over-expenditures are not incurred unless sponsor permission is obtained. There is very frequent reference to this budgetary accountability to sponsors, with a clear organizational focus on ensuring that results are obtained in terms of expending funds for the purposes that sponsors allocate. (Klassen et al., 2019)

Accountability to community is less formal and more interactive and happens at different stages in the life of a project. Village members are involved in the initial scoping of the project which includes developing project targets. They are also involved throughout the project, sometimes in terms of assisting with building, but more often as a key resource in executing the program. Therefore, accountability to the community is not formally expressed in terms of reporting, but more so through the direct involvement of the community in the project and its outcomes. This is important to ensure that the project sustains itself even after its formal completion and after the involvement of RuralDevCo ceases and also to promote the philosophy of *Swaraj*. This interaction with beneficiaries who form the most important stakeholder group is also important in order to maintain transparency and build trust. (Klassen et al., 2019)

A former director of a local office of United Way also confirmed the importance of honesty and transparency.

I think that ... the quickest way to lose the credibility for [a] non-profit organization is trust. For United Way, losing the trust of its stakeholder is the quickest way ... to go downhill, and honesty is how you build trust and I think that has to be at the forefront.

The qualities of modesty, renunciation of selfishness, and contentment are closely related. Patagonia, Inc., exemplifies the quality of contentment with modest returns in that its founders "... did not want 'rampant and senseless growth'.... Thus, they were comfortable with company growth in the 3–5% range" (Merchant & Van der Stede, 2012). The former CEO of the auto parts supplier, referenced earlier, summarized his experience of renunciation of selfishness, or not exhibiting greed, as follows:

I have heard this ... at my [parent] company. They say that please don't think of eliminating your competitor. Don't do that. Let them also survive. Don't think you must have a 100% market share. 50% is okay. 40% is also okay. Find out how much you can invest and for that investment your return on investment and return on sales, keep growing. Don't be selfish and think that the entire market must be yours. Don't do that. So, from an organizational point of view, that is a little bit of a lack of selfishness that came to my mind.

The CEO of a mid-sized company in the business of establishing automatic teller machines (ATMs) offered a different perspective on renunciation of selfishness when working as part of a team comprising of individuals from multiple functional areas.

> I will give you a specific example, I have a sales guy who probably has to go and sell. There is someone else, a finance guy who has got an objective of minimizing the cost of sales. The sales guy will sort of go and spend, and sell at any cost, while there is someone else who is actually working against you to reduce this one. There are apparently conflicting objectives. Now, if you … are completely selfish for your own interest and not looking at the overall organization interest then there will be utter chaos within the organization. I think the renunciation of selfishness becomes pretty much a part and parcel of any team working.

An important element of modesty is a lack of arrogance and a steady focus on the organization's commitments regardless of its achievements in its initial years. This is particularly relevant in today's context where media presence pervades through our society. A former Executive Vice-President of a multinational firm observed that the way the organization thinks and speaks about itself is also an important element of modesty.

> So, modesty is again the way we talk to people…. Do we talk about profits, or do we talk about we being a very sustainable organization? Do we talk about creating shared value for the communities? Do we talk about respect towards water as a community and the way we do things, or do we say we make so much [by way of] profits? Do we say that we are present in so many countries or do we say we are affecting communities in so many countries? As long as we do the latter and we talk about things we are doing to save the planet and the people instead of the profits we generate I think is a where the modesty comes in.

Figure 5.4 is our attempt to conceptualize how these qualities may manifest themselves at the organizational level. Organizational dharma, as a unifying, all-encompassing principle, helps shape an organization's policies and procedures, and management functions. For example, *Satyam*—truth and, by extension, transparency—will drive management to ensure that its accounting and finance policies specify openness with respect to recording, analysis, and disclosure not with the idea of minimal compliance with accounting standards but also in terms of providing forward-looking information that are both positive and negative to guide managers, analysts, and investors in their decision-making. Additionally,

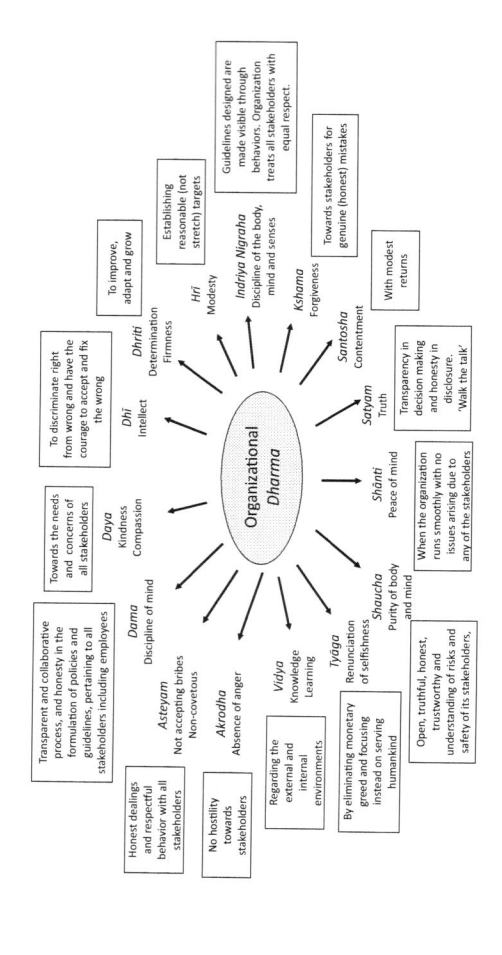

Fig. 5.4 Qualities underlying dharma (*Sources* Bühler [1969] and Bhaskarananda [1998])

transparency will require managers to clearly list all assumptions and decision criteria used when engaged in planning and budgeting, and equally emphasize both good and not-so-good performance when engaged in periodic reporting. The reporting of especially poor performance must not be such that the conclusions are left wide open for interpretation by managers and other users of information.

Similarly, the individual characteristics that represent the universal code of conduct also shape how management functions are designed, developed, and implemented within the organization. For example, *Daya*, understood as kindness/compassion patience, may mean that managers should not put unreasonable and undue pressures on employees. Similarly, *Santosha* interpreted as contentment may influence the target setting process and curb greed. Similarly, *Kshama*, in the form of forgiveness, may shape managerial evaluation processes and reward structures. In turn, this has the potential to increase *Satyam* (truthfulness) among employees, thereby promoting *Dama* (discipline of mind). These can then lead to honesty and openness thereby promoting teamwork and a collaborative rather than a comparative environment within the organization (Kalagnanam et al., 2016).

5.5 Conclusion

Organizations are a collective of individuals and have the potential to experience the same challenges that individuals do when they lack purpose and a set of values to guide the way they live their life. This is particularly important in large organizations where decision-making may be dispersed at different hierarchical levels. The purpose of organizational dharma is to keep the organization together by providing a foundation for decision-making. However, this foundation must be developed by understanding the qualities that underlie dharma—such as kindness or compassion, and truth—and how they might apply at an organizational level. The next two chapters will focus on the enabling mechanisms and obstacles or hurdles in establishing and practicing organizational dharma.

REFERENCES

Bhaskarananda, S. (1998). *The essentials of hinduism*. Sri Ramakrishna Math Printing Press.

Bühler, G., & Müller, F. M. (1969/1886). *The laws of Manu* (Vol. 25). Clarendon Press.

Carroll, A. B. (1990). Principles of business ethics: Their role in decision making and an initial consensus. *Management Decision, 28*(8), 20–24.

Carroll, A. B. (1991). The pyramid of corporate social responsibility: Toward the moral management of organizational stakeholders. *Business Horizons, 34*(4), 39–48.

Cashore, H., Seglins, D., Zalac, F., & Ivany, K. (2016). *Canada Revenue offered amnesty to wealthy KPMG clients in offshore tax 'sham'*. http://www.cbc.ca/news/business/canada-revenue-kpmg-secret-amnesty-1.3479594.

Danak, D. (2010). The divine side of enterprise. *Journal of Human Values, 16*(1), 71–86.

Deshpandé, R., & Raina, A. (2011). The ordinary heroes of the Taj. *Harvard Business Review, 89*(12), 119–123.

Devika, J. (2010). Egalitarian developmentalism, communist mobilization, and the question of caste in Kerala State. *India. the Journal of Asian Studies, 69*(3), 799–820.

Devnani, P. (2009). *Taj goes all out to help victims*. https://www.dnaindia.com/mumbai/report-taj-goes-all-out-to-help-victims-1317014.

Duerr, M. (2004). The contemplative organization. *Journal of Organizational Change Management, 17*(1), 43–61.

Fombrun, C., & Foss, C. (2004). Business ethics: Corporate responses to scandal. *Corporate Reputation Review, 7*(3), 284–288.

Friedman, M. (1970, September 13). The social responsibility of business is to increase its profits. *The New York Times Magazine*.

Hawkins, J. M. (1988). *The Oxford paperback Dictionary*. Oxford University Press.

Hawley, J. (1993). *Reawakening the spirit in work: The power of dharmic management*. Berrett-Koehler Publishers.

Hawley, J. (1995). Dharmic management: A concept-based paper on inner truth at work. *Journal of Human Values, 1*(2), 239–248.

Henneman, T. (2011). *Patagonia fills payroll with people who are passionate*. https://workforce.com/news/patagonia-fills-payroll-with-people-who-are-passionate.

Johnson, E. (2017). We are all doing it: Employees at Canada's 5 big banks speak out about pressure to dupe customers. *CBC News*. https://www.cbc.ca/news/business/banks-upselling-go-public-1.4023575.

Kalagnanam, S., Murphy, W., & Bruni-Bossio, V. (2016). Dharmic management: Principles and practice in organizations. In S. Sengupta (Ed.), *Compendium* on *integrating spirituality & organizational leadership, volume 6: The cultural foundations of organizational leadership* (Vol. 6, pp. 113–119).

Kalidasan, V. K. (2016). A king lost and found: Revisiting the popular and the tribal myths of Mahabali from Kerala. *Studies in South Asian Film & Media, 7*(1–2), 103–118.

Klassen, M., Kalagnanam, S., & Vasal, V. (2019). Managing values and financial accountability: The case of a large NGO. *International Journal of Indian Culture and Business Management, 19*(1), 103–127.

Merchant, K. A., & Van der Stede, W. A. (2012). *Management control systems: Performance measurement, evaluation and incentives* (3rd ed.). Pearson Education.

Noss, D. (2003). *A history of world's religions* (11th ed.). Prentice-Hall.

Parel, A. J. (2006). *Gandhi's philosophy and the Quest for Harmony*: Cambridge University Press.

Pattanaik, D. (2013). *Business sutra: A very Indian approach to management.* Aleph Book Company.

Pava, M. L. (2003). Searching for spirituality in all the wrong places. *Journal of Business Ethics, 48*(4), 393–400.

Pava, M. L., & Krausz, J. (2006). The broadening scope of corporate accountability: Some unanswered questions. *Corporate Social Responsibility, Palgrave Macmillan, New York*, 25–42.

Pruzan, P. (2008). Spiritual-based leadership in business. *Journal of Human Values, 14*(2), 101–114.

Reidenbach, R. E., & Robin, D. P. (1991). A conceptual model of corporate moral development. *Journal of Business Ethics, 10*(4), 273–284.

Sivakumar, N. (2008). The business ethics of Jamsetji Nusserwanji Tata—A forerunner in promoting stakeholder welfare. *Journal of Business Ethics, 83*(2), 353–361.

Tax Justice Network. (2020). *The state of Tax Justice 2020: Tax Justice in the time of COVID-19.* Tax Justice Network.

Teal, T. (1996). The human side of management. *Harvard Business Review, 74*(6), 35–000.

CHAPTER 6

Enablers of Dharma

6.1 Indra's Curse

Once upon a time, Indra, the god of thunder and rains got very angry with human beings. So, he cursed that there will be no rain on Earth for 12 years. Hearing the curse, everyone panicked, because no rain for such a long period meant unimaginable suffering and the death of most flora and fauna, including human beings.

The human beings begged Indra for forgiveness. But Indra said he can't take back a curse once he has given it. So, the only way out was for people to go to Shiva—the supreme being within the Shaivism tradition of Hinduism—and request Him to play His Damru (an hourglass-shaped drum). Indra said, "If the all-powerful Shiva plays His Damru, then it will rain again."

Hearing this, the human beings started walking towards Mount Kailash, the abode of Lord Shiva. But before they could reach Mount Kailash, the cunning Indra secretly reached Kailash and prayed Lord Shiva to not play His Damru for 12 years. Bholenath Shiva said, "So be it." When the human beings reached Kailash, it was too late. Lord Shiva said that He could not play the Damru for 12 years because he had already made that promise to Indra.

Disappointed, the human beings returned to their homes. Slowly, they gave up all hopes for rain. The farmers stopped tilling their soil and

P. Mishra and S. Kalagnanam, *Managing by Dharma*, Palgrave Studies in Workplace Spirituality and Fulfillment, https://doi.org/10.1007/978-3-030-90669-6_6

sowing seeds, because what good would it be when there would be no rains for 12 long years?

But there was one farmer, named Devdutt, who never gave up. He plowed and tilled his land every day, even when there was no rain. Everyone made fun of him. They called him stupid and mad. But he continued to work daily on his land. Three years passed but Devadutt would not give up. He continued with his daily work on his land.

Gradually, the story of Devadutt began to spread beyond his village, and once the king got to know about him. He came to meet Devadutt and asked, "Why are you wasting your time and energy plowing when there won't be any rain for a very long time?".

Devadutt replied, "I know about the 12-year drought curse, but if I don't work on my land for 12 long years, I will forget how to farm. I will lose all my knowledge and skills in farming. That's why I work on my farm … to continue my practice."

Shiva and His consort Pārvati heard this conversation between Devadutt and the king. Pārvati, who is the goddess of fertility and determination, used this opportunity to ask Shiva, "My Lord, after 12 years, don't you think, you too will forget how to play the Damru?" The embodiment of simplicity, Bholenath Shiva immediately realized His mistake and started playing the Damru. Immediately it started raining. And this is how the human beings were saved from Indra's curse.

But this is not the end of the story. After the rains, it was only Devadutt's farm that bore excellent yield. Why? Because he had prepared his farm. The other farmers did not get much yield (until much later) because they had not prepared their land as Devadutt had.

6.2   Importance of Purpose

What is the purpose of statements often labeled as vision, mission, values, or purpose statements? Look good in the eyes of stakeholders? Display that one exists? Use as a guide to run an organization? For Denmark-based Grundfos Holdings A/S, its statement of purpose 'We wish to make a positive difference in the world' (https://www.grundfos.com/sustainability/people/human-rights) is more than just a statement—it is what drives the business. For instance, its main products and services are geared towards enabling and enhancing access to clean water which is a basic need for survival. According to a former Chairman of the Group (and son of the founder), Grundfos does not do anything that has the potential to create any damage to people or the environment. Another important marker of making a difference is its focus on inclusion—hiring a diverse group of employees, including individuals with a criminal record, to give them another opportunity to experience a meaningful existence (Pruzan & Mikkelsen, 2007).

Grundfos, founded in 1945, is primarily owned by the Grundfos Foundation; its other owners are members of the founder's family and employees. The company's philosophy is that profits are simply a means to an end. Similarly, understanding and practicing the company's six stated values—sustainable, open and trustworthy, focused on people, independent, partnership, and relentlessly ambitious—is among its priorities and expectations, which also includes achieving financial outcomes. The attention to financial outcomes is twofold: (1) to sustain the business and (2) to ensure that Grundfos can continue to make progress towards living its purpose.

The company believes that its purpose and values should be firmly ingrained in the minds of all employees—not just managers—and be integrated into their actions and decisions. Over the years, the company has taken several actions to make this possible, starting with formal and informal communication. All new hires go through a process that includes induction, training, and individual and group dialogues so that they understand, recognize, and ultimately internalize Grundfos' mission, vision, and values. The second is role modeling with the aim of developing employees who will not look to managers for instructions; instead, they will take the responsibility for their actions and decisions (Pruzan & Mikkelsen, 2007). The idea here is that values become the foundation for decision-making within the organization. Grundfos management truly believes that honesty and openness are critical to creating an environment that is conducive to instilling the values and developing the right culture; senior management also understands that this is time-consuming and an ongoing process. A critical development going forward, something that is germane to Grundfos' operations, is to formally incorporate human rights issues and the sustainable development goals (SDGs) into its business (https://www.grundfos.com/sustainability/people/human-rights).

6.3   ORGANIZATIONAL PURPOSE

Arthashastra, believed to have been written sometime around 300 BCE (https://www.worldhistory.org/Arthashastra/), mentions that the duty of a king (and by default the kingdom) is welfare (Kangle, 1965); more recently, Peter Senge (1990) has suggested that the purpose of organizations is to contribute to the development of the world, much like the mission of Grundfos introduced above. Corporations perform a variety of functions in addition to providing goods and services to customers (or clients); examples include employment generation, and innovation through new technologies, products, and processes. Ultimately, these activities contribute towards economic and societal development. As long-term living entities, organizations cannot simply focus on achieving a narrow set of objectives (e.g., shareholder wealth maximization); instead, they must focus on simultaneously achieving multiple objectives over time (Bower & Paine, 2017). This undoubtedly requires adopting a broad perspective and working within that perspective. Both individuals and organizations ultimately have a responsibility towards society which is the highest level of stakeholder (Bhaskarananda, 1998); this is because all individuals and entities are part of society (Sankar, 2015). Drawing upon the work of Gichure (2008), Sivakumar and Rao (2010) state that "... social responsibility refers to contributing to the quality of life and to the welfare of society" (p. 504). This is particularly true for a 'responsible' organization that adopts dharma as its core philosophy. Therefore, the natural questions that follow are: "How can this be achieved?" and "How can dharma be instilled within the DNA of an organization?".

According to Danak (2010), organizations may be able to achieve this by liberating themselves from being solely economic entities to recognizing that economic activity is simply the means to an end, rather than the end (Pruzan, 2008), thereby moving from being owner-centric to more nature-centric or society-centric. This idea of liberation aligns with what Einstein referred to within the context of an individual:

> A human being is part of the whole called by us as Universe, a part limited in time and space. We experience ourselves, our thoughts and feelings as something separate from the rest... This delusion is a kind of a prison for us, restricting us to our personal desires and to affection for a few persons nearest to us. Our task must be to free ourselves from the prison by widening our circle of compassion to embrace all living creatures and the whole of nature in its beauty... The true value of a human being is the sense and quality in which he has liberated himself from worldly things. (Chiras, 2009, p. 554; quoted in Danak, 2010)

Bower and Paine (2017) suggest that corporations must transition from being shareholder-centric to company-centered purposeful organizations. They state as follows:

A better model, we submit, would have at its core the health of the enterprise rather than near-term returns to its shareholders.... [Organizations] are economic and social organisms whose creation is authorized by governments to accomplish objectives that cannot be achieved by more limited organizational forms such as partnerships and proprietorships.... The choices made by corporate decision makers today can transform societies and touch the lives of millions, if not billions, of people across the globe. (p. 57)

Such elevation or transformation requires that organizations start right at the top by revising their mission and vision statements such that they strongly convey the purpose and intent both to internal and external stakeholders. It is common knowledge that these statements are often lofty and aspirational in nature and are designed to influence not just senior executives but also employees at all levels within the organization. Consider the following statements (see Fig. 6.1):

Our company's mission is to contribute to the continuous development of the planet through a focus on all relevant stakeholders.
We strive to be a responsible and respectful organization.

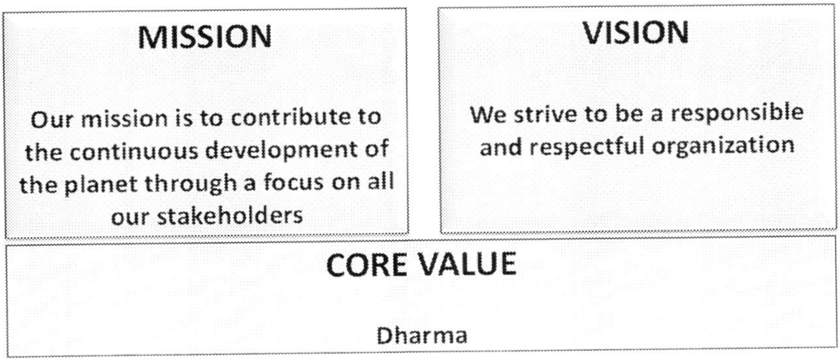

Fig. 6.1 Sample statement of purpose

These statements must force each individual employee to ask the following three questions on a regular basis (Pava, 2007): (1) Who am I responsible for? (2) What am I responsible for? and (3) How can I ensure that I act responsibly in everything that I do? Having to answer these three questions puts the onus on each employee to be accountable towards themselves (Hall et al., 2007) and ensure that they are acting responsibly, by considering the core value of dharma, regardless of the activity (planning, negotiating, reporting, etc.) or whether they are dealing with internal or external stakeholders. The idea is to elevate one's level of consciousness by constantly adhering to the core value of dharma. The key question, then, pertains to how organizations can develop and instill dharma within the DNA of each employee; the rest of the chapter attempts to address this question.

6.4   INSTILLING DHARMA—ENABLERS

According to Sivakumar and Rao (2010), organizations are making efforts to rehumanize the workplace; they observe as follows:

> The shift in focus to business vision, values, character, and ethics has been the first step in rehumanizing the workplace. A new set of values is emerging in the business world, which includes diversity, participatory management approaches, systemic and holistic models, a focus on process, business ethics, social responsibility and care for the environment. (p. 506)

A combination of external, individual, and organizational factors contributes towards instilling the desired core philosophy within any entity.

External Factors

An important development over the past 50 (especially the past twenty) years has been a change in expectations pertaining to corporate responsibility (Cooke, 2010; Warhurst, 2005), coupled with the increasing demands from a variety of stakeholder groups including the community, developmental agencies, activist and lobby groups, watchdog agencies, media, and other similar stakeholder groups (Bekefi et al., 2006; Holzmann et al., 2003; Vogel, 2007; Wartick, 1992). The bottom-line, according to several scholars, is that companies, especially the large ones, can continue to exist only if their values are in alignment with those of the society at large (Dowling & Pfeffer, 1975; Holzmann & Jørgensen, 2001; Magness, 2006; Schuman, 1995).

Two important global developments are the United Nation's sustainable development goals (SDGs), which encourage governments and other organizations (including corporations) to pay attention to societal-level goals (https://sdgs.un.org/goals), and the global reporting initiative (GRI) which is an "… independent, international organization that helps businesses and other organizations take responsibility for their impacts, by providing them with the global common language to communicate those impacts" (https://www.globalreporting.org/about-gri/). One other significant development, both in Indonesia and India, is mandating corporate social responsibility (CSR). Indonesia mandated CSR in 2007; however, this was "limited to companies which have an impact on natural resources" (Waagstein, 2011, p. 460). In contrast, India's mandatory CSR policy, which is enshrined within the Companies Act (2013) requires all companies, that meet one of three financial criteria, "… to contribute at least 2% of the average net profit earned during the three immediately preceding financial years towards CSR …" (Rajeev & Kalagnanam, 2017, p. 93).

The mandatory CSR policy in India—enforced via Section 135 of the Companies Act—specifies the broad parameters of what defines CSR and includes guidelines with respect to implementation, disclosure, reporting, and governance mechanisms. With respect to governance, companies that meet the criteria are required to establish a CSR Committee consisting of three or more members of the Board of Directors, and the committee is charged with the responsibility of developing a CSR policy, recommending CSR projects, and overseeing the implementation of the projects. A final requirement pertains to disclosure and reporting, wherein companies must provide details of their CSR policy, composition of the CSR committee, and an annual report of the CSR activity (including details of the projects undertaken, amounts budgeted and spent, direct and overhead expenses, and unspent amounts). Additionally, companies are required to prepare a responsibility statement confirming that the implementation and monitoring of CSR activities are in compliance with the company's CSR objectives and policy. These requirements have the potential to push companies to carefully consider the idea of responsibility.

Other external factors include the conscious and increasing attention to human rights, environmental regulations, the development of a variety of standards developed by the International Organization for standardization (ISO) such as the ISO 9000 family of standards pertaining to quality management and the ISO 14000 family of standards pertaining to environmental management, and ethical guidelines developed and enforced by a variety of professional bodies covering accountants, engineers, lawyers, etc. The following observation by a former CEO captures the role of externally imposed standards.

> I find slowly these [systems] are becoming documents of dharma in one way, though it is called a quality system. If you consider TS16949 to which automotive companies swear, it talks of measuring literally everything – customer compliance, inventory turns, of course, profitability, safety, statutory requirements, are you breaking any law of the Government etc. Then there is the ISO 14000, which talks of pollution, which talks the environmental concerns etc. If you put all these things together, and if you really implement those things, yours will be an ethical company, a dharmic company and still you will have your certificate and still you will have your profits etc. So, to answer your question, I think the framework is there. If you really go into it, I think the compulsions have been dharmic in nature for putting these things and making companies commit to do these things.

External stakeholders are also an important enabling factor as articulated by a senior executive.

> On the external front, it is also important that the external stakeholders like probably corporation's investors who invest in these companies, might have their own ways of looking at these things. [However], if they have the same value systems as the company, or if they understand the implication of following dharma of the company and understand the long-term benefits of following it, they can possibly enable the process of following it in the company.

Individual Factors

Any organization is a collection of individuals, and it is these individuals who are assuming and playing various roles within their organization. It is therefore important to recognize and understand that individual dharma is also an enabling mechanism to foster organizational dharma. According to an ancient scripture, Taittirīya Upanishad (Chinmayananda, 2008), 'practice your dharma' is the advice that the ancient Gurus gave to their disciples soon after they had completed their education and were ready to enter the next phase of their lives. What did they mean by dharma?

> [It includes] all those fundamental values of life which are universally good at all places and at all times; which form the rock-bottom foundations of all efforts at moral rearmament and all edifices of ethical perfection; which constitute the moral stones for all temples, churches, mosques, synagogues, and *gurudvārā-s*; which are the eternal duties of every man who wants to live up to the full dignity of the human and strive consistently to grow into his fullest stature as a Godman in this very life. (Chinmayananda, 2008, p. 90)

This means that individuals must develop a set of beliefs or a value system that guides their thought processes and their actions on a day-to-day basis. Building upon the foundations of her belief systems, Dr. Carol Franklin, the former Head of Human Resources, Swiss Re Insurance and the former Chief Executive Officer of the World-Wide Fund for Nature (WWF)—both in Switzerland—declared as follows:

> I will only work for a company that has good products that make the world a better place. The idea is that the product itself has to be worthwhile; it has to be in alignment with my spiritual view of life, which is caring for and being responsible for the earth and its inhabitants. (Pruzan & Mikkelsen, 2007, p. 158)

All the qualities underlying individual dharma (see Sect. 4.5 in Chapter 4) can be part of an individual's value system but really it is up to each individual to prioritize certain qualities and nurture them using a variety of familiar tools and techniques, such as meditation, introspection, being associated with a spiritual master, association with right- and like-minded people, yoga, or even a walk in the park or by the water. It could also mean remembering the moral stories that our grandparents read or narrated to us. Our research participants identified several individual-level qualities that they believe are important to practice regardless of time and place.

Clarity of thought and equanimity are important qualities that allow an individual to remain calm and composed even in difficult situations, thereby being able to handle difficult/conflict situations without losing composure. A senior journalist observed that equanimity is more.

> ... mental, personal, it results from a certain maturity of mind, a certain experience in life, knowledge which one has gained through precedence or past events, interacting with people, studying and analyzing similar situations that have occurred in the past etc. but more important is all of us have to keep learning every day, how to face dilemmas and how to come out of the dilemma, how to decide when you are faced with a dilemma with a clear conscience which is not going to hurt anyone, that is extremely important.

Practicing equanimity also requires an individual to understand their ego and keep it in 'check'. An entrepreneur explained the importance of understanding ego using the context of awards received or positions/titles offered.

> I will use an example, I do not ever look for awards, I don't – it is not important to me, it is not interesting to me. I see it as an opportunity to do better because of doors that it opens. I am in a situation where I am feeling a sense of self-importance, so I have been given a chairmanship or I am leading a group, or I am leading a new endeavor. I ask myself 'why are you doing this? What is the reason, what is the purpose'? What about ego? It is always about checking in with myself not to say you are proud of your work because you have done your best so as to say 'wow, that is pretty impressive and then resting in the glory'. I am cognizant over my years of understanding that for me the role of leader is not a title, it is the responsibility that has been given to me with whatever the situation is that I am always learning, open, always be able to assess with a full open heart and open mind.

Another, and perhaps an extremely important, quality is integrity or authenticity which subsumes qualities such as truth and honesty and is practiced by consistently 'walking the talk', which many of our research participants identified as being extremely important. According to Zsolnai (2016), authenticity is a social virtue which enhances trust in an individual. The following passages capture the thoughts of multiple research participants regarding the impact of practicing integrity.

> So, I think it is about having a certain set of principles and living by it day in and day out and that is when everyone, all the stakeholders around

you clearly see that this is what you stand for. My experience is that people generally respect it.

Another enabling mechanism is that 'ambiguity is something which is very difficult, I tell you something and do something else'. I tell in my house that you should not lie and when your call comes, I tell my daughter to tell you I am not there, so this ambiguity is what people judge.

The second enabler is as I said, ignore the world – you are not here to change people, you are here to believe in what you think is right and, if you continue on that path, things automatically start giving you space. Over time the ecosystem starts respecting you, okay, this person is like this. I do not even drink in an alcohol company, I am teetotaler. Nobody will force you to drink because they know that he doesn't even drink tea, coffee, Coke, Pepsi or whatever else. It is not about alcohol or anything else, it is about non-sustainable foods. So, people will start giving you space in their own lives and that is the biggest enabler, so that is what I believe, your belief becomes the biggest enabler then.

It is common knowledge that, in almost every organization, individual employees interact with peers, superiors and subordinates and with other individuals that belong to external stakeholder groups (suppliers, customers, regulators, etc.). Moreover, oftentimes these interactions may consist of negotiations at an individual-to-individual level even though the interactions ultimately affect the organization. What becomes relevant then is understanding the other person's perspective which can result in mutual respect for one another. Freeman and Gilbert (1988) capture this thought as follows:

> If managers start with the principle of 'Respect for Persons', then those individuals with whom they interact will get respect. It means seeing individual customers and employees as whole and complete, functioning persons, capable of making choices, listening to reason, enjoying the work they do, feeling happy, sad, angry and joyous, and trying to find meaning in their lives. (adapted from a quote in Sivakumar & Rao, 2010, p. 507)

A desired outcome from nurturing the individual factors is a conscious shift to focus inward and develop an internal locus of control (LC) so that individuals perceive a greater sense of control over events in their life (Reddy & Kamesh, 2016). Drawing upon the work of Trevino (1986), they observe that individuals with an internal locus of control are likely to:

… behave more ethically because they are more likely to perceive the connection between their own behavior and the outcomes produced by that behavior. As a result, they are more likely to take responsibility for the outcomes of their actions. (Reddy & Kamesh, 2016, p. 111)

The key, for any individual, is to internalize the values and relentlessly practice them just like Devdutt, the farmer in the story narrated at the beginning of this chapter.

Organizational Factors

External factors are often a significant driver of change; similarly, individual factors are important to understand the driving forces and adapt as necessary. However, transformation at an organizational level requires the implementation of a variety of mutually reinforcing elements (or components) to hold the collective together and steer the organization in the right direction. We label this set of mutually reinforcing elements as a management control system. A variety of alternative frameworks of management control exist (Malmi & Brown, 2008; Merchant & Van der Stede, 2017; Simons, 1994); Fig. 6.2 captures the ideas from these frame-

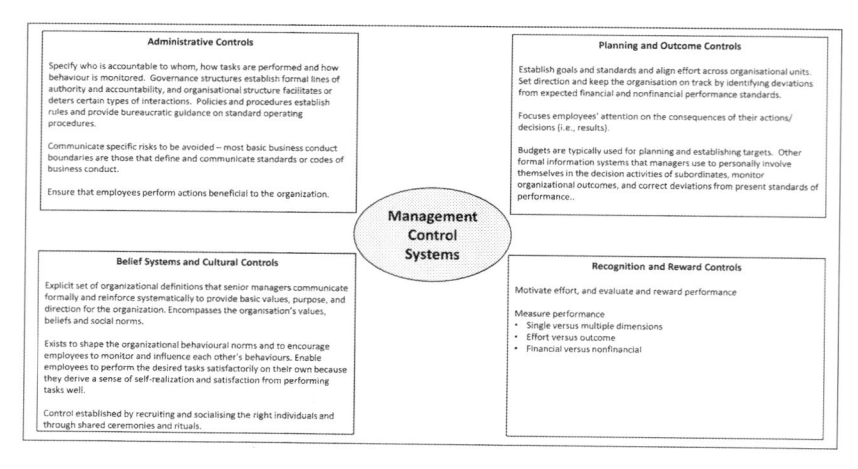

Fig. 6.2 Alternative management control frameworks (*Sources* Malmi and Brown [2008], Merchant and Van der Stede [2017], and Simons [1994])

works. Hawkins (2005) uses the term management control process and notes that it

> ... includes those means by which senior management (1) influences behavior and guides an organization toward achieving its mission, (2) assures that the organization is progressing satisfactorily toward the mission, and (3) assures that the mission is still the preferred one to pursue. (p. 1)

Regardless of the specific management control framework or model that an organization chooses to adopt, the important roles of a management control system include providing direction and support to employees to achieve its objectives, motivating them to take the right actions, and establishing a system to provide relevant information for decision-making and monitoring progress (Hawkins, 2005).

The task of instilling dharma within the DNA of an organization places emphasis on developing, nurturing, and sustaining the belief systems and cultural controls to create an inclusive, open, and transparent climate within which employees feel comfortable, fearless, and motivated, and work together in an open and honest manner (Senge, 1990). It is also about goal congruence which means ensuring alignment between the goals of individual employees and that of the organization (Anthony, Govindarajan, & Dearden, 2007). Previous studies and our research participants identified a variety of mechanisms, tools, and techniques, which are discussed blow and captured in Fig. 6.3 (which also lists the external and individual factors).

Leadership
Several scholars suggest the important role and influence of leadership (Abernethy et al., 2010; Pandey et al., 2015; Schein, 1992). Over the years, scholars have developed a variety of leadership styles, including servant leadership (Greenleaf, 1977); spiritual leadership (Fry, 2003; Pruzan, 2008); authentic leadership (Walumbwa et al., 2008); transformational leadership (Kouzes & Posner, 2012); ethical leadership (De Vylder & Opdebeeck, 2016); responsible leadership (Zsolnai, 2016); and sāttvika leadership (Alok, 2017). Although each of the leadership models may have one or more elements that align with our conceptualization of organizational dharma as articulated in the previous chapter, servant leadership appears to be the most aligned model. "Servant leaders empower

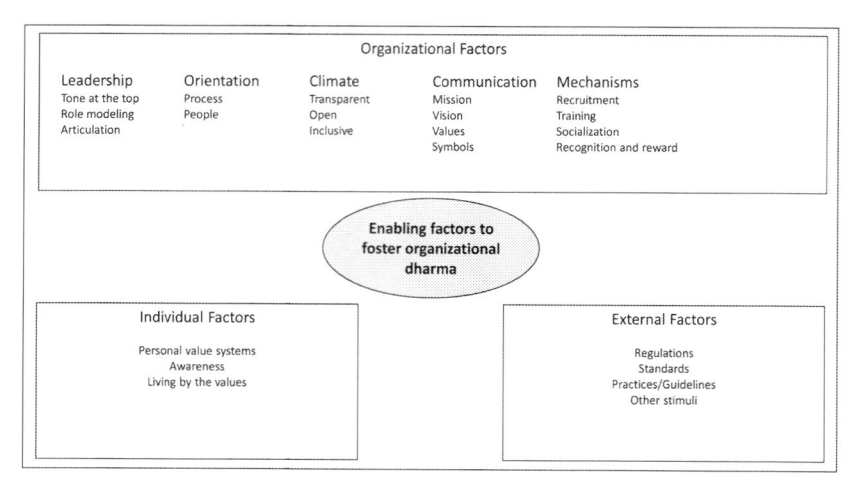

Fig. 6.3 Enabling factors

and develop people; they show humility, are authentic, accept people for who they are, provide direction, and are stewards who work for the good of the people" (Van Dierendonck, 2011, p. 1232). Regardless of the specific style of leadership, what is more important is that the relationship between leaders and their followers is such that it appeals to the followers' value systems, is respectful, inspirational, and transformational rather than transactional (Burns, 1978; Yukl, 2013).

Our research participants identified two important roles for leaders in instilling dharma within the DNA of organizations: (1) articulation and communication of values (including the non-negotiables) and (2) role modeling. A senior journalist with a national media group articulated the importance of a top-down approach to this process, combined with the tone at the top.

> Absolutely and it has to come from the top. 'Yathā rājā tathā prajā', meaning 'as is the king, so are the citizens'. Therefore, the top leadership, the chairman, the MD, the board of directors, if those top officials are able to not only follow a certain dharma but also show to the company and the employees and other stakeholders that they are indeed following a certain dharma, that is extremely important. It has to be demonstrated; as they say, 'Justice should not only be done but it should be seen to be

done'…. The showcasing is not to take any pride in doing what one is doing or for publicity purposes; it is to send out a message which will rekindle the interest in a large number of people.

The CEO of a company in the business of establishing ATMs stressed the importance of communicating especially the non-negotiables.

I think the biggest enabling [mechanism] to my mind is to – right from the beginning – at least let people know that these are the value systems that you would like to operate with and by and large you will never compromise with those value systems, whatever be the result at the end of the day. Once you sort of let people know what your value systems are and what is the red line that you have drawn for yourself, I think that over a period of time it sort of gets established that you are not going to cross the red line, whatever be the result.

According to Klassen et al. (2019), role modeling is one of the most significant elements in shaping an organization's culture. A former diplomat, one of our research participants, reinforced the importance of role modeling as follows:

A boss leads by example. I mean if a boss tells people to come on time and himself or herself comes in late it will not work…. We have a saying in our … embassies abroad, 'an embassy is the ambassador'. The complexion of the embassy, regardless of whether there are 500 people, 200 people, or 50 people, changes with the ambassador. It is a reflection of his personality. So, if the boss is compassionate, people will tend to be compassionate. If he is rude, people will tend to be rude in his organization. If he is punctual, people will tend to be punctual. It is amazing how a boss's personality rubs off on the organization.

Another research participant, an individual with over 25 years of management experience, and a 'spiritual seeker', highlighted the importance of creating a sense of belongingness within an organization and emphasized the role of the leader in doing this. The outcomes, resulting from creating such a sense of belongingness can be truly rewarding.

I will not quote the name, but I will just tell you, that in one garment unit, there was a sudden huge order for export. Okay, these people worked overtime and they were prepared to even forgo overtime payment from the organization. They said they did not want the overtime, but they said they wanted our organization to achieve this. So, we will come, we will achieve this. And they started working two shifts and they were not expecting anything in return. They just wanted the company to finish this and see that this is executed. Of course, in the end, everybody gained. They were given their dues and everything and they were so happy, that 'despite us not asking we were given'. So, this kind of a situation happens only when everybody is practicing dharma.

Recruitment and Training

Value-based or dharmic organizations have the potential to attract potential employees; according to Verschoor (2006), they may in fact be necessary not just in attracting employees but also in enhancing their productivity. According to Word (2012), it is important that employers assess a potential employee's individual (personal) values to enhance their contribution to the workplace.

> ... the greatest organizational goals are realized when the goals and values of the organization are in agreement with the spiritual values of the individual.... She goes on to note that individual spirituality may guide individuals to choose careers or organizations that are congruent with their individual beliefs rather than trying to act out spiritual beliefs through just any organization. (Kalagnanam & Venne, 2015, p. 8)

Instilling dharma can be a strong enabler in terms of building a strong ethical culture. With respect to this point, Sivakumar and Rao (2010) observe as follows:

> The process of building the culture involves the steps of selecting appropriate personnel, the rewarding of ethical behavior, checks on unethical behavior, training the members in the values of the organization and inspiring the members to practice ethics through intrinsic motivation. The characteristics of the culture would be the values, which the members would have cultivated, and their strict adherence to it, thus leading to a culture, which promotes ethical behavior. The final outcome of this culture would be the ethical practices exhibited by all the members of the organization as a whole. (p. 518)

The nature and extent of training are important issues to consider. In their research, Klassen et al. (2019) found that employees in a large value-based organization spent approximately 10% of their time participating in technical and values-based training in their first five years. This training included classroom sessions, observation, and experiential learning. The reiteration of values on a continuous basis, if done properly, can address any 'slippages' in an organization in terms of the knowledge and practice of values. According to a retired executive of a nationalized bank, it is important to ensure that by the time organizational dharma percolates from the boardroom to the shopfloor, "it gets broken down into doable and non-doable [items]" which might resonate better with employees at different levels with the hierarchy of especially large organizations.

Our research participants reiterated the importance of recruitment, onboarding, and training. The general manager of a large construction company highlighted the role of recruitment and onboarding as follows (slightly paraphrased to align with the flow of the discussion):

> All employees who join the company go through induction. One of the topics covered in the induction is the culture of the organization. I have been in this group for the last 26 years. So, I am thoroughly imbued with the company's culture, and we tell new employees what is expected of them. In our dharma the first and foremost is customer satisfaction – the customer is king, there is no doubt about that. My company has always been looked upon as the company which is very averse to disputes and arbitration. We do get a lot of repeat jobs due to excellent relations with clients.
>
> When we select employees also, we try to take from some similar back-grounds – large companies, our competitors who have a similar work culture but modified to suit our dharma. We have our annual days where the promoters come and talk, they reach out to the employees. Some of the very friendly practices towards the employees – we don't transfer them left and right as other companies do. We take care of them. Since we are still a private limited company answerable only to the promoters a lot of leeway is given on employee benefits. So, customer satisfaction and integrity we are very-very strict. Not told openly but it is understood by everyone, that integrity is one issue on which you can get sacked on the spot, irrespective of your achievements.

Recognition and Reward

An important element of any management control system is a system of recognizing and rewarding desired performance. Scholars in the area of performance measurement and reward systems have suggested several alternative approaches to managing this element. Questions raised include what to measure (e.g., effort versus outcome, and financial versus nonfinancial indicators), how frequently to measure (daily, weekly, quarterly, annually), what to recognize (e.g., effort, outcome, or a combination of outcomes), and how to recognize (through financial rewards or other means of recognition).

Simons (1994) suggests that managers have two important levers at their disposal which, we believe, can be used to instill dharma into an organization's DNA. The first such lever is belief systems which include a set of mechanisms that senior managers can use to reinforce their organization's basic values, purpose, and direction. The second lever is boundary systems which identify specific risks to be avoided and communicate this through mechanisms such as codes of conduct. The organization's recognition and reward system can be further superimposed on the two levers to reinforce values and minimize (if not eliminate) risks while, at the same time, motivating employees (Hawkins, 2005). The motivational aspect is important and necessary because only spiritually evolved individuals can be expected to work without expecting anything in return for fulfilling their duties towards their employer (Kalagnanam & Venne, 2015). Such individuals practice what Chakraborty and Chakraborty (2006) called 'nishkāma karma' or detached involvement and experience intrinsic motivation by practicing the values simply because it is the right thing to do (Easwaran, 2009).

The former general manager of a construction company captured the importance of recognition as follows:

> I think it would require what we call a Sadhu – [a spiritually evolved person] – to think 'I don't care even if I am not appreciated, I will still do the work the right way and this is the way it ought to be done and I will do it'. Most of us are ordinary mortals who need the feedback once in a while: 'you are on the right path, you are doing a good job'. What would happen – if that is not there – I won't say that the person will do things wrong but then he doesn't live up to his potential; the productivity falls and probably the lack of quality or the cost overrun or delays in work would not hurt him that much. He feels what difference does it make anyway.

The performance evaluation system of a large values-oriented NGO located across India

... focuses on a blend of technical accomplishments and personal characteristics. Attributes such as devotion and hard work, personal discipline, behaviour, cooperativeness with peers and seniors, integrity and loyalty, collectively accounted for between a third and 40% of the evaluation; the remaining 60% to two-thirds was accounted for by characteristics such as technical competence, willingness to learn, attendance, ability and achievement of results.... For [this NGO], compensation was important but not seen as a significant motivating factor where employees were looking to perform in order to achieve monetary reward. Interestingly, although advancement offers higher compensation, interviewees discussed advancement as an opportunity to 'give back to the community' or 'make a difference'. (Klassen et al., 2019, p. 117)

A similar system exists in a medium-sized business, as articulated by its CEO.

There are two aspects of the performance appraisal. One is clearly [that] there is the achievement against certain stated goals (labelled as Scale A) which you have created at the beginning of the year. Then there is the adherence to the values that you do, that is the softer aspect (labelled as Scale L). ... So virtually there is a scale of A1 to A4 and L1 to L4. So, if you are an A1 and L1, then that means that you are not only a great achiever you are also an exemplary leader. Say, for argument's sake, that you are an A1 and L4; then you are quite a disaster. You may be an excellent achiever but if you are a terrible leader; that is not something which is ever encouraged. Quickly an A1 L4 would find his way out of the organization.

With respect to recognition and reward, Rosanas and Velilla (2005) caution readers (and leaders) that

... a control system reduced to a system of explicit incentives is ethically unacceptable. It depersonalizes the human being by denying her the opportunity of basically performing a personal action. Besides, and with the same philosophical basis, such systems ignore the possibility for such persons to develop their technical and moral values by not making any appeal to them. (p. 93)

Similarly, Sivakumar and Rao (2010) emphasize the importance of not just rewarding ethical behavior but also sanctioning ethical transgressions

(Singer, 1992); this second point was reinforced by one of the participants in our study, a former executive of a national bank, as follows:

> If the organizational values systems are being breached, it does not matter what is the value; the punishment is crystal clear.... Number two, you are not doing any favor to the organization by following the value system; it is one of the key terms with your [employment] with the organization.

Orientation

Both the mission and vision statements presented earlier in this chapter (see Fig. 6.1) support a process orientation rather than a results orientation. Such an orientation aligns well with the notion that results are secondary and only a means to an end. It is, of course, crucial to remember that people are the ones who develop and engage in activities processes. Therefore, people orientation perhaps precedes process orientation. Individuals, who make a sincere attempt to follow the path of dharma, are ideally suited to the idea of process orientation because they

> ... resolve to go on tending their garden even if they get no rewards at all. Every day they bring fresh water, pull out the weeds, and look after everything very carefully (Easwaran, 2009, p. 221). Such individuals are expected to remain calm in all situations and surroundings regardless of whether the results/outcomes of their actions may be a success or a failure, and behave in accordance with a uniform set of qualities irrespective of the environment they are placed in and the challenges that come along their path. (Kalagnanam & Venne, 2015, p. 5)

A process orientation cannot be limited to the operations within functional areas like supply chain, production, or human resources. Instead, it must be broader in scope and cover both the technical and softer aspects of an organization, as explained below by a middle manager in a large, global organization.

> I mean, when I say process and systems it is not just towards delivery, it is also about knowledge, creating knowledge, the entire value system, not taking bribes, bringing tolerance in the system, mapping people, understanding, sense of empathy with each other. The process needs to take into consideration – all these aspects of it – and not just be a mechanical (i.e., one plus one is equal to two) – it is not a binary flow everywhere. The

process needs to have a very efficient way of working which also includes the softer way of management and that I think becomes very very crucial.

According to Duerr (2004, p. 53), "[c]ontemplative organizations tend to place a high value on the process with which they work, with a level of non-attachment to outcome that might be considered quite unusual in other organizations." Non-attachment to outcome is essentially the same as what Chakraborty and Chakraborty (2006) call 'nishkāma karma' or detached involvement and is considered critical to achieving a sense of liberation or 'moksha' according to a variety of scriptures, most notably the Bhagavad Gita or the Song of God (Chinmayananda, 2000).

Duerr (2004) illustrates how a Brazilian food service company approached the mission as stated earlier in this chapter.

> They shut down their factory and brought a thousand people together for four days to reinvent and strategically envision the future together, from every level. [They] also brought in customers. And as they did that, they deepened their awareness of their relationship to society, and the next step was to redefine their whole contribution to society. They changed their whole product line away from foods that created obesity in Brazil to foods that are based on what they found was their core capability, which was … the ability to create health.
>
> As they did that, they then changed their structures from a hierarchy to self-organizing teams, created a consciousness of all the information for everybody so everybody has access to all information and financial data. (pp. 54–55)

This example highlights how a redefinition of the organization's contribution to society (could we say mission?) influenced its product development decision, organizational structure, and values (especially transparency).

The focus on people and organizational culture does not diminish the importance of process by any means; rather it increases the probability of success at the process level because people are the drivers of process. Efficiency, effectiveness, productivity, and other similar measures are still important because they reduce waste and optimize the use of resources. Carrying out processes in an efficient and effective manner is also part of an individual's responsibility in every organization! Measuring the easily measurable results in a process-oriented environment, on the other hand, is useful only to assess effectiveness and alter processes as necessary. Explicit incentives tied to (financial) results, as is common in most profit-seeking organizations, are unacceptable in organization that strives to manage by dharma—they defeat the purpose of such an organization!

6.5   Conclusion

Organizational transformation is a continuous process that requires careful and constant attention especially when society is changing rapidly. However, change is not easy and individuals or organizations with weak foundations will be swayed easily depending upon which direction the winds are blowing. The process of instilling dharma within the DNA of the organization is no doubt a difficult task but not impossible. We believe the task may have become somewhat easier because of the external forces that are compelling organizations to 'behave' but clearly that is not enough. Every organization is a collective of individuals and the collective is an entity in itself; consequently, individuals have to make their own efforts, and the collective has the important task of steering the individuals so that the collective can function in a responsible manner. The most important point to remember is that change requires constant and sincere effort much like our friend Devdutt who plowed his farm knowing that there may be no rainfall for 12 long years. The moral of that story is to not stop putting in the effort when the going becomes tough. It is also important to note that instilling dharma within the DNA of an organization is far from flicking a switch to turn on the light in a dark room for the darkness of arrogance, ignorance, and complacence is within each one of us and likes to remain there for a long time!

References

Abernethy, M. A., Bouwens, J., & Van Lent, L. (2010). Leadership and control system design. *Management Accounting Research, 21*(1), 2–16.

Alok, K. (2017). Sāttvika leadership: An Indian model of positive leadership. *Journal of Business Ethics, 142*(1), 117–138.

Anthony, R. N., Govindarajan, V., & Dearden, J. (2007). *Management control systems* (Vol. 12). McGraw-Hill Boston.

Bekefi, T., Jenkins, B., & Kytle, B. (2006). Social risk as strategic risk. *Corporate social responsibility initiative* (Working Paper, 30).

Bhaskarananda, S. (1998). *The essentials of Hinduism*. Sri Ramakrishna Math Printing Press.

Bower, J. L., & Paine, L. S. (2017). The error at the heart of corporate leadership. *HBR'S 10 MUST, 165*.

Burns, J. (1978). *Leadership*. Harper and Row.

Chakraborty, S., & Chakraborty, S. (2006). The "Nishkam Karma" principle: Its relevance to effectiveness and ethics. *IIMB Management Review, 18*(2), 115.

Chinmayananda, S. (2000). *The Holy Gita*. Thompson Press Ltd.

Chinmayananda, S. (2008). *Taittiriya Upanishad*. Central Chinmaya Mission Trust.

Chiras, D. D. (2009). *Environmental science*. Jones & Bartlett Publishers.

Cooke, D. (2010). Building social capital through corporate social investment. *Asia-Pacific Journal of Business Administration, 2*(1), 71–87.

Danak, D. (2010). The divine side of enterprise. *Journal of Human Values, 16*(1), 71–86.

De Vylder, G., & Opdebeeck, H. (2016). Indian spiritual traditions as inspiration for ethical leadership and management in Europe. In *Ethical leadership* (pp. 85–105). Springer.

Dowling, J., & Pfeffer, J. (1975). Organizational legitimacy: Social values and organizational behavior. *Pacific Sociological Review, 18*(1), 122–136.

Duerr, M. (2004). The contemplative organization. *Journal of Organizational Change Management, 17*(1), 43–61.

Easwaran, E. (2009). *Essence of the Upanishads: A key to Indian spirituality* (Vol. 1). Nilgiri Press.

Freeman, R. E., & Gilbert, D. R. (1988). *Corporate strategy and the search for ethics* (Vol. 1). Prentice Hall.

Fry, L. W. (2003). Toward a theory of spiritual leadership. *The Leadership Quarterly, 14*(6), 693–727.

Gichure, C. W. (2008). *Ethics for Africa today: An introduction to business ethics*. Paulines.

Greenleaf, R. K. (1977). *Servant leadership: A journey into the nature of legitimate power and greatness*. Paulist Press.

Hall, A. T., Bowen, M. G., Ferris, G. R., Royle, M. T., & Fitzgibbons, D. E. (2007). The accountability lens: A new way to view management issues. *Business Horizons, 50*(5), 405–413.

Hawkins, D. (2005). Introduction to the management control process. *Harvard Business School Teaching Note*.

Holzmann, R., & Jørgensen, S. (2001). Social risk management: A new conceptual framework for social protection, and beyond. *International Tax and Public Finance, 8*(4), 529–556.

Holzmann, R., Sherburne-Benz, L., & Tesliuc, E. (2003). *Social risk management: The World Bank's approach to social protection in a globalising world.* The World Bank.

Kalagnanam, S., & Venne, R. (2015). Management control in a spiritually–charged organisation. *International Journal of Indian Culture and Business Management, 10*(1), 1–15.

Kangle, R. (1965). *The Kautilya Arthashastra, Part I, II and III.* Motilal Bnarsidas.

Klassen, M., Kalagnanam, S., & Vasal, V. (2019). Managing values and financial accountability: The case of a large NGO. *International Journal of Indian Culture and Business Management, 19*(1), 103–127.

Kouzes, J. M., & Posner, B. Z. (2012). *The leadership challenge* (5th ed.). Wiley.

Magness, V. (2006). Strategic posture, financial performance and environmental disclosure: An empirical test of legitimacy theory. *Accounting, Auditing & Accountability Journal, 19*, 540–563.

Malmi, T., & Brown, D. A. (2008). Management control systems as a package—Opportunities, challenges and research directions. *Management Accounting Research, 19*(4), 287–300.

Merchant, K. A., & Van der Stede, W. A. (2017). *Management control systems: Performance measurement, evaluation and incentives* (4th ed.). Pearson Education.

Pandey, A., Chattopadhyay, D., & Bose, S. (2015). The impact of leaders' spirituality at work and their reputation on teams' spiritual climate. *International Journal of Indian Culture and Business Management, 11*(4), 473–495.

Pava, M. L. (2007). Spirituality in (and out) of the classroom: A pragmatic approach. *Journal of Business Ethics, 73*(3), 287–299.

Pruzan, P. (2008). Spiritual-based leadership in business. *Journal of Human Values, 14*(2), 101–114.

Pruzan, P., & Mikkelsen, P. K. (2007). *Leading with wisdom: Spiritual-based leadership.* Response Books.

Rajeev, P. N., & Kalagnanam, S. (2017). India's mandatory CSR policy: Implications and implementation challenges. *International Journal of Business Governance and Ethics, 12*(1), 90–106.

Reddy, A. V., & Kamesh, A. (2016). Integrating servant leadership and ethical leadership. In *Ethical leadership* (pp. 107–124). Springer.

Rosanas, J. M., & Velilla, M. (2005). The ethics of management control systems: Developing technical and moral values. *Journal of Business Ethics, 57*(1), 83–96.

Sankar, A. (2015). *Environmental management.* Oxford University Press.

Schein, E. H. (1992). *Organizational culture and leadership.* Josey-Bass.

Schuman, M. C. (1995). Managing legitimacy: Strategic and institutional approaches. *Academy of Management Review, 20*(3), 571–610.

Senge, P. M. (1990). *The art and practice of the learning organization*. Doubleday.

Simons, R. (1994). How new top managers use control systems as levers of strategic renewal. *Strategic Management Journal, 15*(3), 169–189.

Singer, A. (1992). Creating ethical cultures. *World Executive's Digest, 13*, 72–75.

Sivakumar, N., & Rao, U. (2010). An integrated framework for values-based management–Eternal guidelines from Indian ethos. *International Journal of Indian Culture and Business Management, 3*(5), 503–524.

Van Dierendonck, D. (2011). Servant leadership: A review and synthesis. *Journal of Management, 37*(4), 1228–1261.

Verschoor, C. C. (2006). The value of an ethical corporate culture. *Strategic Finance, 10*, 21–23.

Vogel, D. (2007). *The market for virtue: The potential and limits of corporate social responsibility*. Brookings Institution Press.

Waagstein, P. R. (2011). The mandatory corporate social responsibility in Indonesia: Problems and implications. *Journal of Business Ethics, 98*(3), 455–466.

Walumbwa, F. O., Avolio, B. J., Gardner, W. L., Wernsing, T. S., & Peterson, S. J. (2008). Authentic leadership: Development and validation of a theory-based measure. *Journal of Management, 34*(1), 89–126.

Warhurst, A. (2005). Future roles of business in society: The expanding boundaries of corporate social responsibility and a compelling case for partnership. *Futures, 37*(2), 151–186.

Wartick, S. L. (1992). The relationship between intense media exposure and change in corporate reputation. *Business & Society, 31*(1), 33–49.

Word, J. (2012). Engaging work as a calling: Examining the link between spirituality and job involvement. *Journal of Management, Spirituality & Religion, 9*(2), 147–166.

Yukl, G. A. (2013). *Leadership in organizations* (9th ed.). Pearson.

Zsolnai, L. (2016). Responsible leadership and reasonable action. *Ethical leadership* (pp. 35–51). Springer.

CHAPTER 7

Hurdles/Challenges

7.1 Bhishma's Dilemma

Mahābhārata, one of the epics that most Hindus are familiar with, is full of questions pertaining to dharma. Bhishma, whom we have met in Chapter 1 is one of the central figures in this epic. Growing up, Bhishma never enjoyed the love, affection, and guidance of both his parents *together* at any point in his life. This meant that he spent the first 15 or so years of his life with his mother Goddess Ganga and later with his father Shāntanu, the king of what was then known as Bhārat (undivided Indian sub-continent) and whose capital city was Hastināpura.

Shāntanu could see that his son was indeed well-versed in politics, administration, ethics, and the art of warfare and that there was no individual who matched Bhishma's capabilities and personality. He therefore wasted no time in announcing Bhishma as the crown prince. However, Bhishma's destiny had other plans for him. As things turned out, he felt compelled to take a vow of celibacy and declare that neither he nor his progeny would ever stake a claim to the throne in Hastināpura. Instead, he considered that his foremost duty was to protect the throne and serve whosoever occupied the throne in the same manner as he would serve his father. For Bhishma, the foremost criterion was 'the good of Hastināpura' when making any decision.

P. Mishra and S. Kalagnanam, *Managing by Dharma*, Palgrave Studies in Workplace Spirituality and Fulfillment, https://doi.org/10.1007/978-3-030-90669-6_7

Let us fast forward a couple of generations where we encounter three more characters in the epic, the first of which is the blind Dhritarāshtra the current king of Hastināpura and the occupant of the coveted throne. The second is his eldest son Duryodhana and the third is Yudhishtira who is the king's nephew and eldest son of Dhritharāshtra's half-brother Pāndu who was originally appointed as the king. However, due to a mishap, Pāndu renounced the throne, self-exiled himself to the forest and later died when his five sons were still young. Yudhishtira and Duryodhana are the contenders for the title of 'crown prince'.

It appeared to be quite clear that Yudhishtira had the advantage both based on merit and on him being older than Duryodhana. However, both Duryodhana and his father Dhritharāshtra believed that Duryodahana is the rightful heir to the throne by virtue of him being the eldest son of the ruling king and the 'questionable claim' that Yudhishtira was the older cousin. Besides, Dhritharāshtra had his own personal axe to grind because he had always harbored the feeling that he was wrongly bypassed when Pāndu—who was younger—was appointed as the king. Perhaps more important than the personal axe to grind was his blind love for his son; he simply could not imagine offending his son in any way, shape, or form.

Clearly, this decision posed a major dilemma. There was no easy solution because regardless of the decision one party was going to be left feeling deceived and/or cheated. Unfortunately for Bhishma, King Dhritharāshtra was both incapable and unwilling to make this decision regardless of the fact that such a decision falls within the king's scope of responsibility. As the elder statesman and the grandsire in the family, all eyes turned to him for advice on this critically important decision. How can he apply dharma in resolving this situation? By focusing on what is right for Hastināpura? By focusing on the interests of the occupant of the throne whom he visualized has his father? By giving into the claims of Duryodhana? Who ever said practicing dharma is easy!

7.2   What's in a Name?

Let us now turn to a more contemporary setting which also exemplifies blind love and its consequences. What can a name convey to the outside world? A lot, if the name is 'Satyam' which means 'Truth' and when the truth finally comes out in the form of a bombshell for all relevant stakeholders, including over 52,000 employees worldwide. The key player in this story is Ramalinga Raju, a seemingly simple and unassuming person with rural roots who in 1987 co-founded Satyam Computers, a multinational information technology (IT) company that grew to become one of the top five IT companies in India until it abruptly folded after a confession of wrongdoing by Raju. Was this confession a result of guilt, intentional to suffer less punishment, or a genuine display of 'satyam'?

Raju, the darling of his hometown, was a model 'son of the village' who cared for the members of his community and was well liked by everyone. He engaged in corporate social responsibility (CSR) much before it became mandatory via Section 135 of the Companies Act of India (2013) and even earned praise in the form of an award from the Federation of the Indian Chamber of Commerce (FICCI). His pioneering CSR activity was the establishment of the Emergency Management and Research Institute (EMRI) and the emergency number 108 which could be used by citizens to request emergency medical service. All these activities helped Raju accumulate goodwill and win the confidence and trust of people, including government officials, financial institutions, Board members, and many other stakeholders (Nag, 2009).

What was the reality hidden behind this façade of humility, simplicity, and truth? The answer to this question potentially explains the biggest corporate fraud that had been brewing for several years in the first decade of this millennium. What might be the possible explanations for something like this? Unadulterated greed to satisfy a lust for land? Blind love for sons that leads to doing whatever it takes? A desire to look good in the eyes of stakeholders and avoid alarm bells from ringing in their minds? The answer could very well be 'all of the above'. Regardless of the order in which these reasons may have lined up, each fed on the other thereby leading to Raju engaging in activities and transactions that effectively resulted in him siphoning money from the business to satisfy purely personal wants (not needs), hiding behind the 'curtain of truth and trust'. The end result was illustrative of the consequence of falling victim to lust which manifested greed.

Raju's demeanor appeared to have appealed so much to stakeholders that even the start-studded Board did not suspect any wrongdoing until close to the 'end of the game' when he was caught in his self-created web. The lack of transparency by Raju goes completely against the quality of truth, and little or no oversight by the Board suggests complacency and a disregard for sincerely fulfilling a fiduciary duty. There is no doubt that

Raju would have heard the term dharma numerous times starting from his childhood. The question remains—how may Raju have understood, interpreted, and internalized dharma? In other words, what did dharma mean to him?

7.3   A Dharma Breakdown

Most organizations, especially the large ones like Satyam Computers which is now part of Tech Mahindra, develop value statements and ethics policies, establish codes of conduct, have whistleblowing policies and other similar programs in place. Despite these, it is not uncommon to find examples of large mishaps such as financial fraud affecting some or all shareholders of a corporation, tax avoidance or more seriously tax evasion affecting a variety of stakeholder groups, promoting misinformation or fake news which appears to have become popular and prevalent especially in the past decade but one that potentially poses serious societal challenges, or relatively smaller issues such as a departmental manager building slack into the department's budget purely out of self-interest. Why do individuals and organizations engage in such behavior? This is an important question regardless of the nature and/or magnitude of such a mishap.

In Chapter 5, we proposed the dharma triangle (see Fig. 5.3) which suggests thinking about organizational dharma as a goal, as a foundation, and as actions/decisions. The 'goal' is about ensuring that employees understand the principles and qualities that underlie dharma; the 'foundation' forms the underlying guiding framework; and the two together combine to enable individuals to make the right decisions. In other words, organizational dharma manifests itself through the 'actions/decisions' of employees. This means that undesirable behavior displayed by individual employees, or the organization as a whole, is the result of a breakdown in the dharma triangle.

7.4   Instilling Dharma—Hurdles

Similar to the enabling factors, challenges or obstacles also belong to at least three categories: external, individual, and organizational (see Fig. 7.1); this chapter elaborates upon each of them.

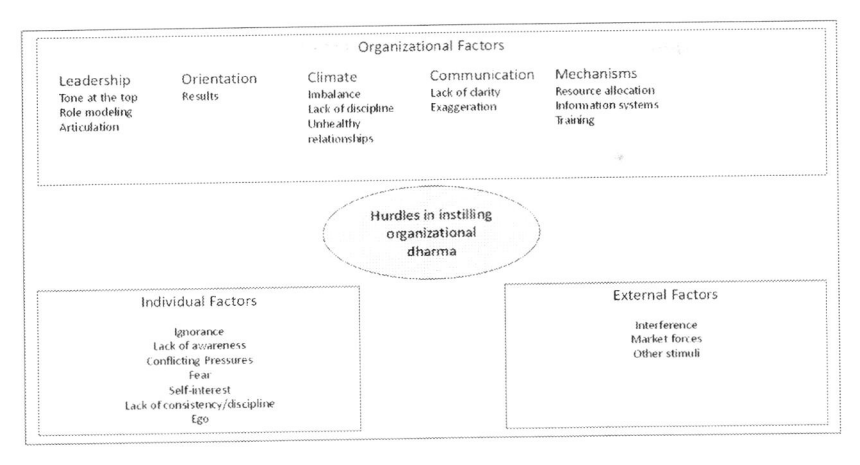

Fig. 7.1 Hurdles in instilling dharma

External Factors

In the previous chapter, we identified several factors such as regulations, standards, and corporate social responsibility (CSR), that can motivate (or enable) dharmic behavior. Can these also become obstacles to pursuing dharma? The answer, sadly, may be 'yes' because these external factors can be very burdensome for at least some organizations and therefore act as hurdles rather than enablers. Other external obstacles may include bureaucratic procedures, lack of alignment with or undue pressure from key stakeholder groups. The CEO of a company articulated his experience of a conflict due to a regulatory agency as follows:

Let me give you a specific example. You want a license for or opening a factory in a particular place and your entire success for the year depends on [its] timely opening … and for whatever good reason, bad reason, the Government which is supposed to give you the license does not give it in time. That is a humungous obstacle. There are short term ways of getting it out. There are people who resort to influencing them, bribing them or whatever way you want to do that. If you don't do it, there is a danger of your spilling over. Now how do you sort of deal with that…. There are conflicts that you come across every single day…. So, I think, managing that is very very tricky, that is where generally the tendency to sort of say, this one time let me just forget about it and let me just get things done.

> But I think the moment you do that … it will come back biting you at some stage. I think conflicts are there all the time. The trick is obviously how you achieve your objectives without you know, compromising your value systems.

Partners along the supply chain can often pose challenges if there is a misalignment of values or if the supplier or customer has considerably greater clout and chooses to exercise their authority. Common issues with existing or potential customers pertain to price (cost), quality, and timeliness which can often be an obstacle, as articulated by the former general manager of a large construction company, and any company that blindly follows the slogan 'customer is always right' may face conflicts.

> If you have customers or clients who are not understanding, who don't accept the fact that good quality takes time and they want you to push through at any cost, then that is an obstacle, you will end up with a product that leaves you dissatisfied. Your role is one [where you have] to give a good project, build a good building and because the client has pressurized you, you have taken short cuts, that leaves you very unfulfilled.

Section 135 of the Companies Act of India, which mandates CSR, allows corporations to implement their CSR projects through their foundations or in partnership with NGOs. Although many companies may comply with the regulations, some may find the policy to be restrictive, unclear, or face difficulties in attracting and retaining personnel to implement meaningful projects (Kalagnanam & Rajeev, Forthcoming). Consequently, for the sake of complying with Section 135 of the Companies Act, such companies may engage in projects simply to 'check off a box'. The former Executive Vice-President of a large global company articulated the challenges associated with being able to execute meaningful CSR projects. These challenges may include lack of public infrastructure—say poor road conditions or limited availability of utilities—in a certain local area.

> If you go through a larger scheme of things, the [bureaucratic] machinery is an obstacle. Suppose I want to do something on a large scale. You need permissions, you need approvals from local authorities and all that. When we do several projects for our company a lot of approvals are required. Say for example, I [find] that at some place electrification is not happening or roads are not proper; I can make capacity with my friends, I can build the

road. So, three of us or four of us unite … and we say we [can] build the road for them. But it cannot happen; I cannot do it. I need approvals. Somebody else will say, give me money or donate it to our firm, [but] what is really happening through that firm or NGO, what is really going to the society, that is a big obstacle. So, we will do in a small way directly, we are sure it happens, it goes to the right person. What we indirectly do through agencies or some other firms or big companies, [we cannot be sure] whether it reaches the [intended] people.

Individual Factors

Merchant and Van der Stede (2012) identify at least three different individual factors that promote unethical behavior: (1) basic dishonesty, (2) ignorance of values, and (3) lack of moral courage (or lack of conviction). Kalesnikoff and Kalagnanam (2012) provide an illustration of basic dishonesty, leading to greed, among a small group of individuals (majority shareholders) in a large global corporation who used the legal and regulatory frameworks existing in small countries to their advantage by 'robbing' the minority shareholders of their rightful share of the financial returns and the host country's government of tax revenue. The idea of basic dishonesty, leading to greed, is also illustrative of the downfall of Satyam Computers.

Individuals who are genuinely ignorant of values may not have the capacity to recognize what is right and what is wrong and may therefore engage in activities with a complete lack of awareness. Two of our research participants introduced two different kinds of awareness problems, one which results from individuals unconsciously going about their daily activities and the other that results from individuals having a tainted view of themselves.

> Okay, you are unconsciously going about with life. That is the actual problem. It is said that when you are conscious of yourself, you will be dharmic. Ah, but you are mostly unconscious though we think we are conscious in the different senses. We are not conscious whether we are being dharmic or not. We don't ask ourselves every time when we are speaking to somebody, am I speaking the right thing, am I speaking the wrong thing. We are largely unconsciously doing many things or automatically doing the things. So, this is obstacle number one.
>
> … no matter what kind of job I did, I always ended up being the acting boss or placed in a position ahead of when I was ready and when I finally

was ready, I had never wanted to be a boss. I thought I will learn on how to be a really good boss and so I prided myself on my humility and my ability to get along great with employees and all that kind of stuff. I was a VP at 37 and by the time I was 40, I was starting to feel like I had all the answers and of course you don't have all the answers no matter who we are. I became more controlling, more of a micro manager. I wasn't an asshole but it wasn't in sync with who I really am and what I espouse. When I was about 41, we embarked on a process where we were trying to change the culture from one of command and control to more inclusive and I was one of the architects of it and I realized that I was kind of part of that 'hierarchical way of being' even though I didn't think of myself that way, so it was huge blind spot. Then we had a bunch of 360s done which is when I discovered – much to my surprise and no one else's (including my husband) – that I had a powerful presence, that I could be intimidating and fiercely intelligent was the feedback I kept getting and so that really upset me because I didn't see it yet I'd prided myself on being self-aware.

A lack or moral courage or conviction, or a lack of self-discipline, may be the outcome of a fear of the immediate consequences of engaging in dharmic behavior, pressure arising from multiple factors such as a conflicting situation, new job and the felt need to impress, and ambition/personal goals. Individuals who face such conflict situations may choose to engage in *adhārmic* activities and justify them. Regardless, the lack of moral courage translates into the inability to transform one's principled or morally correct stand into an action. Justification, or rationalization, is one component of the fraud triangle where the individual engaging in an *adhārmic* activity "… perceives the misdeed as unavoidable or justified" (Phillips et al., 2018, p. 234). The following passages capture such conflict situations.

On a personal level if you are poor, if you are starting up in your career where taking a short cut is a very tempting thing to do maybe it can get you promoted faster and what not, so there again [it is important to think carefully] despite your personal handicap either financially or otherwise.

There can be many obstacles, most important obstacle is the individual – how he feels he should be living. For example, some people have principles [that they live by]. Then, at the same time they feel family is important. If I have to take care of my family, which is one of the things, already I am two steps down, I may compromise. My child is not well. So, there are personal things which can come in the way. If it turns too much in the extreme, it can be harmful. But, individually as a human being when you are working in an environment, you will definitely [have to make some] trade-off.

As a journalist I would often face conflict of interest situations. I am associated with a large number of initiatives [and] I am privy to ... confidential information that is actually newsworthy. Should I write about it or should I not write about it? For me it is a very big dharmasankat [a moral conflict]. If I write about it, I will follow my journalistic principles of breaking news -for me it is news.... But at the same time, I must remember [that] the ... MD or the CEO of that company has trusted me as a friend and shared confidential information with me. Should I not maintain his trust? How can I release whatever confidential information is shared with me? ... I need to balance this and often I ... would wait. In law, there is a term called balance of convenience. Now, where is the balance of convenience? If I were to write this story, who is it going to help and who is it going to hurt and if I were not to write that story who is it going to benefit and who is going to be hurt? I will do that evaluation and I will come to a particular judgement in my own view. Some others may even dispute that judgement but for me it is my personal conviction.

Other commonly known individual factors such as ego, self-interest, interest of family or close friends, lack of competence, personal desires, and the desire to look good in the eyes of those around us, ambition, stress, and personal attitude which may include a 'don't care' approach or a focus on the short term, can and often do lead to *adhārmic* activities. The following passages, paraphrased to maintain continuity, articulate some of these factors.

The impediments which come, I think, are a function of our own ego which all of us have and it rears its head up several times a day. Our own sense of material desires and ambition which very much comes in the way – unfulfilled ambition which then drives the way we think or act, react, feel elated or depressed or get angry. So this basket of desires of ambition – and then I would go even to say greed – all of us have some greed in us – those become the impediments to following your life, the path of dharma. So, dharma is also little bit of truth within or living your life by listening to your conscience and, as I said, our ego and our sense of impressing others in society around us come in the way of that.

If I let my ego lead the way, I will trip and that is not a good thing. It is a hurdle when others with whom I am working may not have the same principles as I do, and I respect that. So, what I must do in that case, is that I must learn how to understand everyone with whom I am working and

> must be open minded to understand where they come from – could there be a cultural background difference, could there be an evolutionary difference relative to their own experiences in life, might there be a self-interest. So, I have had to learn to first and foremost understand the people with whom I am working and sitting at the table and how to not manipulate but really to understand the framework with which I am working and then to be able to speak intelligently and be prepared on the subject matters that I am addressing.
>
> So, there is stress that is a hurdle for lot of people and from stress comes fear. I feel that based out of fear, their decisions may be and their positions may be based out of pressure to perform; I have had that happen where they have not been prepared to take the risk. There is, and I have worked with this too, there is manipulation, there is dishonesty, there is self-interest. Thankfully, not very often but I have come across it a couple of times in a very negative, narcissistic light, and I have to understand that too and how to work with that. That means how do you remove that toxicity – and for the overall good – you have to remove that toxicity.

It is common knowledge that every organization is a collective of individuals who work together to achieve the goals and objectives of the organization. Each link in this web of individuals must do their part and all it takes is a single weak link to disrupt the web. It is much worse when this weak link is an individual who is in a position of authority.

Organizational Factors

We introduced a management control system (MCS) in the previous chapter; an effective system includes a set of *mutually reinforcing* mechanisms in that each individual mechanism should ideally complement the others in the set. Why is such a system required?

> If all employees could always be relied on to do what is best for the organization, there would be no need for an MCS. But employees are sometimes unable or unwilling to act in the organization's best interest, so managers must take steps to guard against the occurrence, and particularly the persistence, of undesirable behaviors and to encourage desirable behaviors. (Merchant & Van der Stede, 2012, p. 9)

The four types of control identified in Chapter 6 (Fig. 6.2)—administrative controls, planning and outcome controls, belief systems and cultural controls, and recognition and reward controls—are equally important for every organization to function smoothly. However, there may be variations in terms of which type of control is emphasized more (or less) and the extent to which individual elements or mechanisms within each type of control is used. According to Chenhall (2003) and (Anthony et al., 2007), the design of a management control system is contingent upon several factors such as the organization's size (Ezzamel, 1990; Kalagnanam & Lindsay, 1999), culture (Martin, 1992), technology defined in terms of workflow (Woodward, 1980) and interdependence across the functional areas (Hickson, Pugh, & Pheysey, 1969), its strategic focus (Govindarajan & Gupta, 1985), and the level of environmental uncertainty (Chong & Chong, 1997; Hoque, 2005) facing the organization.

Uncertainties may result from technological developments, market forces, and even unpredictable events such as the recent and continuing COVID situation. It has been widely reported that organizations around the world have been affected by the recent COVID situation and this has forced them to adjust to the new reality and prioritize accordingly. For some organizations, this may mean significant attention to the financial needs of the organization to the detriment of meeting other goals or employees unable to perform their tasks in a desirable (dharmic) manner. The following passages capture the idea of uncertainty and its potential consequences.

> Internal to the organization would again be pressure coming from your superior and resource constraint. Sometimes you do not get the resources you have asked to carry out a good job- maybe the workers are not properly skilled, or you are not given enough machinery to carry out the job. That could be internal. Not getting the support you are looking for.
>
> Obstacles, I think, it is a contextual thing specifically if you are talking about organizations and their focus on profitability and increasing revenue, specifically it might have issues, I mean practicing the duties of an organization, specifically might also include compliance with regard to local laws, compliance with respect to regulations and compliance with respect to what one would expect a reasonable organization to do with regard to environment. So, there might be a situation where, you know, there is always a financial component, a cost component towards practicing dharma or fulfilling one's responsibility to the fullest extent, which an organization might or might not deem important when it compares it with something as important as profitability for its own sustainability.

Another important factor is the level of flexibility built into the control system. A 'loose' control system will likely promote undesirable behaviors for the simple reason that opportunistic behaviors by self-interested individuals cannot be held back. However, the remedy for that is not a 'tight' system that is very rules and procedures oriented because this can be frustrating for employees and may stifle creativity and innovation, which may be necessary when fulfilling duties towards stakeholders. The need to fulfill duties towards stakeholders should not result in false or misleading communication, as articulated by a director of a not-for-profit organization.

> See, … having been part of a few companies in the IT world, I could see a mad rush for numbers, right? So, you will have to, you are required to amplify things, right? Project things in such a way that it is music to the ears of your customer or whatever, while the actual reality might still be a little different. The marketing team would say, or the sales team would go and say that we can do this project in three months, … we have a whole lot of expertise to do it. What we would eventually end up doing is to slog it out, learn new things because somebody else committed. So, these are situations you will come across in a professional life, which are, which create those small conflicts.
>
> So, obviously there is an organizational vision, focus, objectives etc. and every organization is there to make money, be there in business, all fine and understood. But what is that balance? If something is being projected completely different from what the organization is, then there is a conflict and here is where the concept of dharma to strike that balance is very important. We used to, just as an example, talk about a product which was in our labs, not even market awaited. The pitch that goes out is that we have all these capabilities, all these products just to get business, which is very discomforting for people at the other end. So, how do you deal with such instances?

The lack of balance across and within the four types of controls can pose significant challenges and create hurdles for employees, and the organization as a whole, in acting responsibly or in a dharmic manner. For instance, the danger of focusing exclusively on results is explained by Mahatma Gandhi as follows:

> He who is ever brooding over results often loses nerve in the performance of duty. He becomes impatient and then gives vent to anger and begins to do unworthy things, he jumps from action to action, never remaining

faithful to any. He who broods over results is like a man given to objects of senses, he is ever distracted, he says goodbye to all scruples, everything is right in his estimation and he therefore resorts to means fair and foul to attain his end. (Fischer, 1962, p. 63)

Similarly, an excessive process orientation with little regard paid to outcomes can potentially limit organizational learning.

Leadership is both an enabling mechanism and an obstacle. For instance, a leader's inconsistent behavior and/or prioritization of goals, objectives, and values will naturally send mixed messages to employees. Similarly, regular and/or frequent changes in leadership, as may happen in certain organizations like government agencies or departments, can easily disrupt the stability of the organization's climate and culture as well as the task of instilling dharma within its DNA, as articulated by a middle manager in a large global company.

> … organizational DNA takes, I will say million years to build. The reason I used a very extreme term called millions is because organizations go through a lot of changes sometimes in leadership and the moment there is a leadership change the organization's way of working changes, the DNA starts changing again and that I think is the big-big gap which I see from again putting dharma because dharma needs to go beyond people, beyond leadership.
>
> There must be a bigger vision that the organization has. If those are so clear, then it is very important at an organizational level, this entire path of delivery of all these objectives on the ground gets ingrained [in the minds of] each and every person and when people move out also, the same philosophy needs to continue because the rest of the team understands the entire space of what is happening. So it can be put in only from the top, from the very-very top and every leader who replaces the other leader needs to be similar in understanding the DNA of the organization and also the understanding that if that is the dharma that they have put as an organization or started with one aspect of culture, then they should not change it so often that people will be headless and not understanding the same purpose and get lost here and there.

Other organizational factors include the lack of training or reinforcement of the organization's values and beliefs by the senior leadership team including the Board members, misaligned incentive systems that confuse employees with respect to what is important, bitterness among employees leading to situations where collaboration or cooperation is next to impossible, and a general lack of openness or transparency.

7.5   Conclusion

It is common knowledge that a building with a weak foundation is more prone to collapsing, when a storm hits the area, compared to one with a stronger foundation. Dharma is that foundation both for an individual and an organization, and a breakdown in dharma can result in the individual (Ramalinga Raju) and the organization (Satyam Computers) to collapse. It is therefore important for both the individual and the organization to constantly monitor the foundation and find ways to strengthen it to be able to weather any kind of storm.

References

Anthony, R. N., Govindarajan, V., & Dearden, J. (2007). *Management control systems* (Vol. 12). McGraw-Hill Boston.

Chenhall, R. H. (2003). Management control systems design within its organizational context: Findings from contingency-based research and directions for the future. *Accounting, Organizations and Society, 28*(2–3), 127–168.

Chong, V. K., & Chong, K. M. (1997). Strategic choices, environmental uncertainty and SBU performance: A note on the intervening role of management accounting systems. *Accounting and Business Research, 27*(4), 268–276.

Ezzamel, M. (1990). The impact of environmental uncertainty, managerial autonomy and size on budget characteristics. *Management Accounting Research, 1*(3), 181–197.

Fischer, L. (Ed.). (1962). *The essential Gandhi: His life, work, and ideas; an anthology.* Vintage Books.

Govindarajan, V., & Gupta, A. K. (1985). Linking control systems to business unit strategy: Impact on performance. In *Readings in accounting for management control* (pp. 646–668). Springer.

Hickson, D. J., Pugh, D. S., & Pheysey, D. C. (1969). Operations technology and organization structure: An empirical reappraisal. *Administrative Science Quarterly*, 378–397.

Hoque, Z. (2005). Linking environmental uncertainty to non-financial performance measures and performance: A research note. *The British Accounting Review, 37*(4), 471–481.

Kalagnanam, S., & Lindsay, R. M. (1999). The use of organic models of control in JIT firms: Generalising Woodward's findings to modern manufacturing practices. *Accounting, Organizations and Society, 24*(1), 1–30.

Kalagnanam, S., & Rajeev, P. N. (Forthcoming). Implementing mandatory corporate social responsibility in India: Assessing progress made by corporate and NGOs. *International Journal of Business Governance and Ethics.*

Kalesnikoff, D., & Kalagnanam, S. (2012). Caribbean brewers: Transfer pricing, ethics and governance. *IMA Educational Case Journal, 5*(2), Art.1.

Martin, J. (1992). *Cultures in organizations: Three perspectives*. Oxford University Press.

Merchant, K. A., & Van der Stede, W. A. (2012). *Management control systems: Performance measurement, evaluation and incentives* (3rd ed.). Pearson Education.

Nag, K. (2009). *The double life of Ramalinga Raju: The story of India's biggest corporate fraud*. HarperCollins Publishers India.

Phillips, F., Libby, R., Libby, P., & Mackintosh, B. (2018). *Fundamentals of financial accounting* (5th ed.). McGraw-Hill Ryerson Limited.

Woodward, J. (1980). *Industrial organization: Theory and practice* (2nd ed.). Oxford University Press.

CHAPTER 8

Case Studies

8.1 The Power of Stories

Long ago (roughly 200–300 BCE), in the kingdom of Mahilaropya, there lived a great king, named Amarshakthi. Not only was he an able administrator, but he was also known for his practical wisdom. But alas! He was very sad. His three sons were disobedient, lazy, and totally averse to the very name of learning. The king was worried about the heir to the throne, as his sons seemed to be incapable of governing. All his efforts to provide them with good education had failed. Something had to be done, and soon. In desperation, he held a brainstorming session with his council of ministers.

> Your majesty, basic education itself takes 12 years. And when that has somehow been mastered, there are others to follow; the study of law, economics, management, and human relationships. These have to be tackled and mastered; only then can one become an able administrator.

The king was deeply disappointed. He said, "Gentlemen, I am already in the evening of my life. So, we have no time to lose. This calls for desperate measures."

Then one of his ministers informed him about a certain Vishnu Sharma, who was known among his students to be an erudite, efficient, and empathetic teacher.

P. Mishra and S. Kalagnanam, *Managing by Dharma*, Palgrave Studies in Workplace Spirituality and Fulfillment, https://doi.org/10.1007/978-3-030-90669-6_8

Entrusting the princes to his care may provide a speedy solution to the problems, your majesty.

The king sent for Vishnu Sharma at once and beseeched him to accept his sons as his students.

Revered sir, I humbly request you to instruct them so that they become unsurpassed in their mastery over all matters relating to practical wisdom.

Vishnu Sharma agreed and promised to achieve this goal in a short span of six months. Accordingly, the king entrusted the princes to Vishnu Sharma, who took them to his ashram, as was the practice those days in India. Since the princes abhorred formal education, the accomplished teacher devised a series of stories that were a distillation of the knowledge in the shastras (or texts). He used these stories to teach the princes the necessary rules of conduct and statesmanship.

As promised, the princes too, within six months mastered the art of intelligent living and leadership. Since then, the reputation of Panchatantra has traveled worldwide and become an excellent means of awakening and training young minds.

In his English translation of the Panchatantra, Olivelle (2006, p. 17) quotes Franklin Edgerton (1924) who is supposed to have said:

No other work of Hindu literature has played so important a part in the literature of the world as the Sanskrit story-collection called Panchatantra. Indeed, the statement has been made that no book except the Bible has enjoyed such an extensive circulation in the world as a whole. This may be—I think it probably is—an exaggeration. Yet perhaps it is easier to underestimate than to overestimate the spread of the Panchatantra.

The Panchatantra stories are powerful and have been translated and adapted into cultures across the world.

We think Panchatantra may be one of the earliest documented successful attempts of providing value-based education through stories. Edgerton's attestation of the Panchatantra certainly points to his admiration of the text, but at a general level, it also attests to the power of stories. Stories are very powerful and engaging stimuli. We are all so fond of stories, be it in the form of novels, gossip, or movies. The appeal of stories is universal. In his book, *Changing Minds: The Art and Science of Changing Our Own and Other Peoples Minds*, Gardner (2006) asserts that storytelling is one of the two most powerful tools of changing minds effectively. It is in this spirit that we share a few cases.

8.2   DRINK RESPONSIBLY

... alcohol, unlike popular perception, is not sin. If you look at all great companies, ... all good alcohol companies, they make very good quality products. When you talk about good quality products, there comes good ethics of doing business. Now sugar is also very-very bad. Who would you blame – the guy who [eats] a lot of sweets – [or those who make them]? ... I also have a tendency to indulge, and that is also as harmful or even more harmful, so anything in moderation is always good for the body. The moment you cross the line on anything, it is very detrimental. Now, the same thing with alcohol, you make quality products, market them in a responsible manner and nobody is telling you to drink or not drink responsibly, so it is about an individual's choice to cross a line and instill harm on himself.... I am working for a world-class organization making the best quality products, we also operate in [the] most ambient space. So, I take very great pride in the quality of products. Having said that, the product consumption is not very important to me. If I am working in a bikini brand, I would not have been wearing bikini. Okay. That is the whole point. Sashidhar Vempala, Head of Communications and Sustainability

Pernod Ricard India Private Limited (PRIPL), a wholly owned subsidiary of Pernod Ricard SA, operates throughout India via over 30 bottling plants, two distilleries, and a winery. It serves the Indian and export markets through a wide range of premium whiskies and white spirits including vodka, wines, cognac, gin, liqueurs, and champagne. The unit in Nasik, which includes the winery and a distillery, is a one-of-its-kind integrated risk management and zero pollution, state-of-the-art facility. This unit and the other distillery are the first winery and the first Alco-Bev units, respectively, to receive the FSSC 22,000 certification. Pernod Ricard India is recognized as an industry leader with various honors and awards under its share of achievements, including the prestigious 'Best Places to Work 2021' by BW People and The Economic Times 'Best Places to Work for Women 2021'. The company has also been certified as 'The Great Place to Work 2021' by the Great Place to Work Institute.

Dharma, at PRIPL, is about being and doing right and this overarching principle manifests itself via addressing stakeholder needs and through internal mechanisms. This two-pronged approach is designed to ensure that the organization and individual employees develop and maintain both an 'external' focus and an 'internal' focus. PRIPL is a profit-seeking business and therefore generating profits is an important priority and the company's responsibility towards investors. Having said that, PRIPL believes in creating shared value for the business and local communities in a way that drives transformational growth and development for the country.

Consequently, the society at large is another important stakeholder group and giving back to society is not just a duty or responsibility but a 'requirement' according to Mr. Sriram, Ex-Vice-President of Manufacturing of the company; this thought process aligns with the idea that every individual entity is part of society as noted by Sankar (2015) and every entity must recognize and carry out its societal level dharma (Bhaskarananda, 1998). PRIPL does not believe in contributing to specific funds managed by external agencies or non-governmental organizations (NGOs) and letting these organizations decide how its contributions will be utilized. Instead, it employs a hands-on approach and believes in "directly getting the jobs done" and this happens largely through its foundation—Pernod Indian Ricard Foundation—which is established as a wholly owned subsidiary of PRIPL.

The foundation is committed to the cause of corporate social responsibility around the location of its bottling plants and other units and beyond, and its programs are grouped under the four broad areas of education, healthcare, livelihoods, and water and environment. The Ex-VP is passionate about these interventions and briefly elaborated upon some of them.

> One of the biggest projects we did was in Rajasthan. We went to a village, first we collected data of where the shortage is. We found one of the villages in Rajasthan where there was a huge shortage of water. There were many places – we identified this place where people for the last so many years walked 11 kms to get two buckets of water. Then we found the root cause, there was a lake which was there but as usual somebody had built, somebody had diverted. So, we decided to revive the lake. So, we revived the lake three years back, and this year we were very happy to see that the lake is filled with water. Not only is the biodiversity happening, ... birds

are coming, there are trees grown around the lake area, so it is a whole lot of things that is happening, and the rains have started coming and all that – similar big things are happening. The other thing we found was, which is very intriguing in [some parts of] India, especially in villages, was that girls don't go to school because there are no toilets, so what will they do. It is really sad that their time is 10:00 pm or 6:00 am – otherwise they could not go. When we identified that we went to the girl's school and said that we will provide toilets.

Here we can provide toilets and keep quiet and come back because it is not maintained. So, we employed an organization that would maintain [the toilet] for two or three years with the village's support.... We were happy, when we did a survey the next year, to find a 20-30 % increase in girls going to school because of this. Then, once it becomes sustainable, [we] give it to the village and say that we have maintained and the agency which is involved in construction [will go] once in a while to check. So, some of the small interventions like this, while you can see many billboards and signages in India saying that make a girl child study, it is not happening. [We have to] educate them but we have to enable the processes in organization [and the question is] how will you do that? Then we went to several villages. We went to several organizations and said that let us give some employment to women. Employment will not be in corporate setting but something like give them a sewing machine, give them some handicrafts which they can move. The bigger suppliers – we called them and said source from them. So, for example, one of the villages in Kerala or Karnataka, we asked them make jute bags from recyclable material and got one of the agencies to source from them. So, they did and as a saleable model in both ways, it works – the organizations get a cheap rate, and the villagers also benefit.... So, small interventions like this across but if all big corporates and organizations put together – there are a whole lot of things that we can do to contribute to the society especially when we found that lot of basic amenities are lacking.

Another significant initiative of the foundation is the establishment of a social impact incubator for women social entrepreneurs and changemakers called the We Program. The main objective of this incubator is to "… invest in empowering women and supporting their endeavors and provide them with a powerful opportunity to catalyze not only their economic and social empowerment but essentially that of society at large" (http://pri foundation.com/incubator).

The external focus of Dharma at PRIPL is backed by strong internal mechanisms beginning with the key question of 'why the company exists'; this question speaks to the company's existence beyond profitability within the overarching principle of being and doing right. If this is not well-defined, "people will go in different directions, and they might choose different ways" according to Mr. Sashidhar Vempala, Head of Communications and Sustainability. Once this is decided, several steps are necessary to instill Dharma in the DNA of the organization. The first step involves articulating the priorities in a clear and consistent manner and reinforcing the message through regular communication.

> Do we talk about profits, or do we talk about being a sustainable organization? Do we say that we are present in so many countries or do we say we are affecting communities in so many countries? ... There must be a bigger vision that the organization has. If that is clear, then it is very important at an organizational level, this entire path of delivery of all these objectives on the ground gets ingrained with each and every people and when people move out also, the same philosophy needs to continue because the rest of the team understands the entire space of what is happening, so it can put in only from the top- from the very-very top and every leader who replaces the other leader needs to be similar kind of people, understanding the DNA of the organization and also understanding that if that is the Dharma that they have put as an organization or started with one aspect of culture, then they should not change it so often that people will be headless and not understanding the same purpose and get lost here and there.

The next step involves establishing the path to enable the organization is moving towards answering these high-level questions. These steps are important to ensure that (1) that these are not subject to change whenever there is a change in the organization's senior leadership and (2) each and every employee clearly understands the high-level goals as well as the path to achieve them.

> The instilling part is process and systems ... so if you put string processes and systems, then, I mean, when I say process and systems it is not just towards delivery, it is also about knowledge, creating knowledge, the entire value system, not taking bribes, bringing tolerance in the system, mapping people, understanding, sense of empathy with each other; everything the process needs to take into consideration – all these aspects of it – and not just be a mechanical – one plus one is equal to two – it is not a binary flow everywhere. The process needs to have a very efficient way

of working which also includes the softer way of management and that I think becomes very-very crucial.

Employees are also a key stakeholder, and it is important for any organization to validate the commitment towards employees not just through words but also through the actions that align with those words (meaning walking the talk). According to Mr. Shrikant Lonikar, former Chief Human Resources Officer (CHRO), Pernod Ricard South Asia, Gulf, and India, the employee-management relationship is a two-way street in that management often tells the employees about how much the organization cares for its employees and the employees, in turn, tell management how much they are committed to the organization. The true test of any such statements is when one comes face-to-face with the demands of life and unforeseen situations, like the pandemic, that require one to make difficult decisions. "Thankfully, Pernod Ricard made a public announcement at the beginning of the pandemic that people will be the single most important priority of the company and thankfully we lived by that promise in letter and spirit."

It is perhaps common knowledge that a happy employee is a productive employee. To this end, the former CHRO articulated an employee-focused program called 'Ananda' which is rooted in the philosophy that 'employee' is just one of the many roles that a human being plays.

People cannot compartmentalize their different roles they play in personal, social, and professional life. Any event in one part of life invariably impacts other. Also, engaging someone is not possible. People choose to be engaged or not. Engagement happens either when one derives happiness from what one is doing or that activity fulfills one's goals in some way. Engaging a group of people/employees, hence, is even more difficult. With this in mind, Ananda focuses on 8 different dimensions of life of a human being, i.e., Social, Intellectual, Occupational, Physical, Financial, Emotional, Spiritual, and Environmental. If a person is able to fulfill their goals in all or most of these areas most of the time, they are likely to be happy. This happiness will lead to engagement in what they choose to do, and such engagement may make them more productive. In the organization, people need to feel a sense of excitement about their work. To realize this vision, we allow our employees to choose a project of their choosing, even projects unrelated to job. Also, it is by the employee and for the employee. It is a voluntary. For example, we have had somebody who was passionate about photography, so we provided them with resources to pursue it with passion. We allow people to pursue it for as long as they want to. After a year or two of pursuing a particular passion, if somebody wanted to switch to something different or withdraw, we allow that. If anyone does not want to do anything under Ananda, they are not motivated or forced. It is their choice. The purpose of the Ananda program is that people get to try different things that they get excited about, like it is a play. We provide framework, resources, and any support they may require. We support them without imposing any regulations or expecting any deliverables from the projects. This sense of no obligations and freedom to choose keeps our employees happy, and consequently, more productive at work. In addition, Ananda is open for families of employees, who can do all that an employee can under Ananda. Engagement of family in the work and workplace provides a different perspective to employees. If they see their family members are happy being part of the organizational initiatives in some way, they feel more happy and grateful to the organization. All three factors, focus on 'whole' human being, voluntary nature, and involvement of family, make Ananda unique and effective.

Qualities such as intellect, kindness, compassion, absence of anger, and modesty manifest themselves in PRIPL's processes and ways of working when dealing with both internal and external stakeholders. With respect to this point, the Head of Communications and Sustainability observed as follows:

Now, organizational forgiveness comes at a place where you are allowing employees to learn from their mistakes and grow. So, employee is a key stakeholder and that [forgiveness] comes in when [we] see a particular employee has a gap in delivery, we invest more time in training this employee and bringing him up to a particular knowledge level- that is only when you identify him as a good potential. This identification process is called tolerance for me. So, if the organization becomes tolerant, it is exhibiting forgiveness there. So, that is how I see this particular value being played at an organizational level in terms of stakeholders or even suppliers; sometimes, you have good suppliers who have the capability of delivering good quality products to you, but they do not have the resources today. Now do we invest in partnership, giving them long-term deals and have identified them as key partners irrespective of their inability to deliver on time and leaving us in lurches many times? So, do we at that time say, no, you have not delivered as per my expectations. You are not a good supplier or a vendor, so that is the way I see tolerance coming in and capacity building of key potential partners or employees or other stakeholders.

8.3 DYING WITH DIGNITY

... I was working in spiritual care at City Hospital and there were a lot of people, elderly people, who were in hospital for extended periods of time. They did not have much hope for the future, as some of them were at the end of their lives. It seemed to be a very unhappy way for this group of people to die. At around the same time, my mom died, and for her, there was so much love, there was so much goodness at the end of her life. I had a really strong feeling that everyone should have that care, that everyone should have that kind of loving care, if not with family, then with staff who choose to take really good care of people at the end of life. Jennifer Keane, Co-founder

Prairie Hospice Society is a non-profit community organization that is committed to enhancing the quality of life of those facing advancing illness, death, and bereavement and fulfilling its mission to ensure access to quality end-of-life support in Saskatoon, Canada. It is fashioned after a model of "hospice without walls" and provides trained volunteers to assist clients of all ages to complete their life's journey where and how they wish to. This is particularly relevant and important given that individuals who have few family members and/or friends to support them may experience feeling isolated as they approach the end of their lives. A recent study found that clients of Prairie Hospice experienced reduced social isolation and a greater sense of control and dignity when they were matched with a volunteer to provide support (Pham et al., 2020).

Over the course of its decade-long journey, Prairie Hospice has expanded to offer three different programs: (1) Hospice Without Walls, where clients are matched with a specific volunteer for regular visits, (2) Hospice Now, which is intended to meet urgent and temporary non-medical supports, respite, and household-related services to clients, especially transportation and (3) Bereavement Support, which focuses on providing support to the family and caregivers of deceased clients. Its team includes a Board of Directors who provide governance, a small team of paid staff who manage the operations and a large team of specially trained volunteers who provide the service to clients.

Dharma, at Prairie Hospice, manifests in different ways starting with the purpose of the organization which is to help a vulnerable section of the society (Bhaskarananda, 1998). Often, clients, volunteers, and Board members may all underestimate the impact of working in palliative care and how relationships and connections get formed that then can lead to a feeling of loss and grief—this is not a process that is suitable for everyone. A clear articulation of the purpose and its understanding by relevant stakeholders, especially volunteers and Board members, is important to ensure that the 'Prairie Hospice Team' delivers on this purpose. A lack of understanding of the organization's purpose, by any individual including a Board member, can potentially cause the individual to be demotivated in a short period of time, as articulated by the Board Chair: "Oh absolutely, so when we recruit board members, we have to be dead honest with them about what they are taking on and occasionally people think they know what they are taking on and they say, oops, no, this is not for me. Not that I don't believe in Prairie Hospice; ... I will give you a big donation and this is as much as I can do for you."

Prairie Hospice's guiding principles, as articulated by the founders, include compassion and deep care, service, action, right words, right speech, and right action and these are critical for at least two reasons. First, the clients (people nearing their end of life) are very vulnerable and therefore need special care; moreover, this is a stressful situation for family members or close friends and supporters, and they also require additional supports. Second, the actual service is provided by a team of volunteers who are in close contact with the clients and their families; the degree of humanness that the volunteers must practice is perhaps one of the most critical elements of service delivery. In other words, volunteers (especially) are required to follow what Jack Hawley refers to as Dharmic Management which means "... bringing together that truth with you when you go to work every day. It's the fusing of spirit, character, human values, and decency in the workplace and in life as a whole" (Hawley, 1993, p. 1).

The Chair of the Board of Prairie Hospice added 'peace of mind' and 'knowledge and learning' as two more important attributes that can help volunteers in responsibly and successfully fulfilling their roles. "We do look essentially for people with kindness and compassion who want to learn and know and who have the curiosity about life and also the peace of mind." Regardless, an important question that is asked of potential volunteers is their reason to volunteer and any hint of selfishness in their response raises a red flag. "So, we will be looking for ... people who are less likely to be doing this for themselves and more out of a motivation that is rooted in kindness and compassion but, in some ways, you also need to have the intellect in order to be able to speak about that and to

rationalize it for yourself." Understanding this and developing the experience to be able to recognize such individuals and developing a process
to recruit the right volunteers took time for Prairie Hospice.

Three additional important action items contribute significantly
towards developing the right mindset among volunteers the first of which
is training which was initially developed by one of the founders and
included elements of mindfulness in every session.

> It was the necessity to be looking deeply at our own experience, to be
> checking in, to be using wise speech, listening very deeply; also, there
> was, as part of the training, appreciation for spirituality in all of its forms
> and diversity and also a deep look at our own grief, our own losses and
> suffering. So, the training as Phil and I created it, was very rich in personal
> development, and again, I cannot say how it has changed but those were
> the foundational aspects of the training: personal and spiritual development
> of each of the volunteers in order to offer this very precious kind of help
> to people at the end of life.

The second action item is matching volunteers with clients and the
volunteer coordinators take time to look at suitable "matches" so that a
volunteer and client have certain compatibilities. A higher level of compat-
ibility can go a long way towards increasing the comfort level of the client.
The final action item is a 'check-in' with volunteers—especially the new
ones—two to three times a year so that the volunteer coordinator gets
to get some feedback and more importantly to ensure that the volunteers
are in the right frame of mind. This is particularly important because of
the nature of the clients and the service to be provided, both of which
can emotionally drain a volunteer. The Chair of the Board articulated this
'check-in' process as follows:

> … in the contact that we have with volunteers, often after the first kind of
> client experience, the volunteer coordinator will do an interview with the
> volunteer, go through what happened, where they felt it worked-it didn't
> work, if they want to change, what kind of clients they are assigned to,
> so there will be a kind of review of it but that review will also involve,
> what did it do to you and how did it affect you and if it did, how did
> you resolve some of those feelings, how did you deal with it? So, it is a
> check-in with the volunteers that we do quite regularly. Two or three times
> a year, of course during COVID, things are different but there are sessions
> where the volunteers come together where we do volunteer appreciation,

> but we also ask people to talk about their successes, we ask them to talk about their feelings and we check-in with them, how are you doing, what is this experience like for you, it isn't simply tick-tick-tick, did you get all the things done that you were supposed to for this client or did the client think you were a great volunteer, it is also how was it for you and how was this experience for you which would be very different than if I were being hired to do a job. My boss [in my previous job] never asked me how it is going for you other than is anything getting in the way of you getting the job done and with the volunteers it would be a much more check-in with the emotional and a psychosocial state than it would be 'did you have the resources you needed to get them driven to one place or another or help them do a hobby at home or whatever it is they are doing.

The principles guiding Prairie Hospice, like in any other organization, are there to guide the organization in translating its purpose into action in a responsible manner and deal with ethical dilemmas along the way. The founders and the Board Chair identified one common dilemma which can easily arise because of the close relationship between a volunteer and their client. As articulated by one of the founders, "… it is not unknown that when someone dies, and [when] they have received wonderful care that they want to give a gift to the person who has served them." This is an important ethical dilemma especially when the client wishes to give a large gift such as jewelry or even leave an inheritance. Prairie Hospice addresses this via a policy which says that volunteers are not to accept gifts and also by constantly reminding the volunteers about this during their training. According to one of the founders, establishing boundaries is important and this aligns with one of levers of control that are available to management (Simons, 1994). Another ethical dilemma that the Board Chair mentioned pertains to the organization taking a stand on policy changes at a societal level.

> … the one that would be front and center and comes to mind right away is MAID- medical assistance in dying and we have struggled long and hard about what our position is on this. Some of our volunteers would come to us and they are deeply religious or spiritual and they would say the idea of someone wanting to end their life with medical assistance is appalling to me and abhorrent and I do not want to be involved and I think they are sinning. Others would say I really support this, my own grandfather did this, I would move heaven and earth to get them access to medical assistance in dying if that is what they wanted. So we had to

have a look at that and we have revised and had examined many times our policies on medical assistance on dying and have taken a stand that some people would say is a cop-out but potentially we have trained our volunteers in exactly who in the system to connect the client to who would be helpful and support them if that is their choice and we make sure that all volunteers feel able to do that, they could not volunteer for us if they could not refer the client to the appropriate resources, but we have also said that we neither support nor oppose medical assistance in dying and we have also told the volunteers that if they themselves are okay with it and if their clients asks them to be with them in their medical assistance in dying journey including serving as a witness or being with them, that is entirely their choice. It has happened but when you think of ethics there is a really big ethical dilemma for many of us that we need to answer in our own hearts but how do we as an organization tell our client?

8.4   Towards a Better Community

... every time I chat with somebody ... it opens up my brain to think, like, I am always thinking what else can we do? How else can we be better? Just looking at that list of Dharma it is like we say we are accessible but are we. Are we really? I think what else are we missing, what else can we include, we say we are open to all diverse people, it doesn't matter on one's sexual orientation, religion or gender or that sort of thing but are we really open to accepting people? I guess, like I said before, what are those barriers that we are blind to, that we can't see, and I guess it will come to our awareness if somebody tells or if somebody has an experience and we find out about it. Then it comes to more communication to be better and serve better. I am personally always striving for it. Neysa Gee, Coordinator

Saskatoon Community Service Village is a collective of six non-profit agencies that are all housed in a single location and is committed to improving the lives of individuals in local community. The Village achieves success through the synergies derived from co-location and collaboration, and the four principles that guide its functioning include accessibility, collaboration, leadership, and diversity. With respect to the synergies, they are an outcome of several potential benefits that a co-location model offers. According to Clark (2002), the anticipated benefits as identified by the partner agencies at the time included joint programming, planning and policy dialogue; space, equipment, and technology sharing; human resources benefits; building design and central location; broad community partnerships and community leadership; and mentorship and incubation. With respect to the four guiding principles, the Village's coordinator reflected upon them as follows:

> … so those guiding principles were created in the beginning with the input from the agencies so everything that the Village has created stems from the conversation with all of the agencies, so they together have brought together, how do we as a group of organizations stand together and say who we are, so we want to be accessible that everyone who walks in the door, we want to make sure that we are diverse and we represent all of those individuals in our city, we want to make sure there is collaboration together and that we are providing the best leadership that we can.

A former Executive Director of United Way of Saskatoon, who was actively involved during the conception phase, echoed the importance of collaboration and the building of relationships along the journey towards establishing the Village.

> … how it happened was through relationships, people taking the time to talk to one another, it wasn't driven specifically by one organization, it was more of a collective but at the same time everybody brought different strengths to the table. We took the time…
>
> … many organizations have tried to do what we did but they tried to rush it … people didn't take the time to actually develop trust. … the length of time it took us to work through the development of the vision, the engagement with the community, the re-engagement with the community, the working with each of our organizations, the coming together in creating a new model, it was at least 3 years and we took a day or two days every month to bring our leadership group together to work through a lot of the relationship building that was necessary to be able to continue to move forward. So, trust, time, and communication [matter]…

Another important factor during the initial days was tolerance towards risk.

> Lots of stuff went sideways … we had no money at one point and the builder wasn't going to keep going, they were going to walk if we weren't able to come up with the money. … I have a lot of risk tolerance. I guess you would never raise money if you didn't believe that, and other people didn't. We were standing there, and I said it will work out, I will talk to the builder, and we would bring a couple of other businesspeople to that

meeting and even if we have to get a bridge loan, we will do it. Then a number of donations were received. That gave us some more time, money came in. we were able to pay our bills.

An important observation is that the six agencies that are housed in the Village facility have been in place since the Village's inception over 20 years ago, which leads one to potentially conclude that the pioneers carefully considered what it would take to keep the members of the Village together, and that the formal (and informal) mechanisms that were put in place have worked well.

> Because the partner agencies have been here since the beginning, I think if there were to be any type of conflict or disagreement with the village guiding principles to what the agency has, probably it would be difficult for the agency to stay in the building. All of the agencies, their executive director or CEO, we have a meeting every two weeks, we plan, and we collaborate together. I think they are all supportive of the village guiding principles.

Saskatoon Community Service Village identifies with several qualities that underlie Dharma; these include kindness and compassion, truth, peace of mind, forgiveness, contentment, and knowledge and learning. These are particularly relevant because of the diverse nature of clients and their needs, and therefore the variety of services provided. A rather interesting approach to thinking about these qualities, as articulated by the coordinator, is that many of these qualities are also relevant to the clients themselves.

> … when individuals come for counseling or they are working through trauma, we want them to be truthful, to have peace of mind or wanting them to purify the negative energy or the negative experience they have experienced, which would create purity. I don't know if that would resonate with purity of body and mind, but definitely it would allow for forgiveness and maybe absence of anger as well because total forgiveness would be acceptance, absence of anger…. I would say … a lot of it is learning either a new thought process or a new way of looking at things in order for people to heal. I would say those qualities would be what the village would want to instill in individuals coming to our facility to access services and also, we want people to be aware of what we offer as well. It is interesting that I have never thought of these qualities that an agency or an organization would be able to, I don't want to say advertise

but acknowledge and allow these qualities to shine through, that people would think of these qualities if they thought of the agency.

The Village recognizes that putting the guiding principles into practice takes considerable effort, especially given that many of the clients belong to the vulnerable section of society and face barriers that many others do not experience.

> We always talk about what are the barriers that individuals face before they even get to us. So, we want to be open and accessible to individuals coming to us and how can we eliminate those barriers, we want to offer that kindness and compassion in a way that makes it easier for individuals to reach out because sometimes it is not always easy picking up the phone or sometimes, they don't have a phone or sometimes they don't have a car. So, what are those barriers that people need to overcome that make it more difficult to access. We are always talking with the agencies to ensure that there are accessible services provided. Some agencies have reached out to the community and have moved their service delivery in different locations, so some of them have offered counseling at the library … [or at a local pharmacy]. Some go to schools, some of them to other community centers to make it easy for people to access. So … just reaching out and also just working with other agencies in the city as well, so the Food Bank, the Friendship Center, which is the soup kitchen, working with other agencies so [that] it is not so difficult to access us.

An important challenge for the Village as for any organization that is developed on a co-location, collaborative model is ensuring that the collaborative model continues to function as it has in the past. An important indicator of success of collaboration is the fact that the Village has retained its member agencies for the past twenty years; yet it is not free from challenges. One such threat is a pandemic like situation which limits interaction, potentially restricts access to financial and other resources, and the very ability of the Village to fulfill its mission through providing services to clients. Another threat is competition among agencies for financial, human, and volunteer resources. With respect to competition for financial resources, the village coordinator observed that this had not yet happened in any significant way and one important reason for this is the fact that the executive directors of many of the agencies had served for a long period of time and maintained the collaborative approach that existed right from the village's inception. However, this can change, as articulated by the coordinator.

> Potentially it could, yeah. It could for sure even though the board of directors of the village are very adamant to explain to the executive directors, the purpose of the village, why we are here, the purpose of meeting together and not to stay in the little huddle or your bubble or your little office but to actually come together and work together. So, because of the village board is made up of representatives from the agencies, the village board reps go back to their agency boards and share any information that we discuss at the village board and their agency boards. So, the communication does happen which is probably why it has worked for so many years, which is great but that could be a risk in the future, for sure.

The lack of involvement of the village coordinator in the recruitment processes of the individual agencies as well as the currently existing governance mechanisms may also pose challenges. The village coordinator is very much aware of the potential for such a risk and the necessity to address it.

> So that is that could be a heightened risk when hiring the new person and if they decide, I am not really into this way of thinking or this philosophy, these guiding principles, I don't agree with for whatever the reason could be, that could be an issue. The village board has said in order to be here as an agency you are agreeing to abide by these guiding principles and having said that, we sign and the agency signs a lease to rent space. With their lease there is also a co-location agreement explains this is what the agency is expected to do, this is what the village will provide, this is our purpose and why we are here; it is definitely shared with them, and they are aware of it. So, if they still decide beyond that it is not really in our best interest as an agency, our agency is taking a different turn, then there probably would have to some discussion with the agency and the board of directors in how that would play out, I don't know what the outcome would be of that because that is thinking in the future but there would definitely be a discussion with the board and the agency.
>
> There are no set terms in the by-laws that say that you will serve two, three-year terms or that sort of thing. It is mostly as long as the person wants to be on the village board. So sometimes there is high turnover because the individual leaves their agency board. So, if they leave their agency board, they often leave the village board. Having said that the individuals on the village board don't necessarily need to be on their agency

board, they can recommend a representative to represent their agency. Mostly those individuals have previously been on the agency board, so they are aware of the agency and what they stand for and their by-laws but some of them have finished their term and decided to stay with the village board and some of them decide not to and then they appoint a new representative from the agency board. We have talked about just within the past two years may be, sometimes for the agencies, it is difficult to recommend two people. So, we have discussed that maybe we should just do one individual and then have six people from the community as board members. But that hasn't come to fruition yet but that might be something for the future.

8.5   Conclusion

Stories are a powerful medium to educate and the three case studies presented in chapter provide rich examples of how a business in the alcohol industry and two small community-based organizations establish and practice dharma in their own ways. The idea of dharma as a duty towards the community is rooted in both Prairie Hospice Society and Saskatoon Village, and the key element is one of educating employees and volunteers about the guiding principles so that these principles are solidly entrenched and become the foundation for decision making. This is critical because both organizations serve vulnerable clients. Both organizations experience conflicts or dilemmas and attempt to overcome them through a constant reinforcement of the guiding principles. Pernod Ricard India Private Limited (PRIPL), a global corporation in the alcohol industry, promotes the idea of responsible drinking to its customers. As a profit-seeking business, it must wrestle between the competing interests of shareholders and society in general. Internally, the company has developed a strong foundation and continues to ensure that it is continuously reinforced through a variety of mechanisms that focus both on people and process.

References

Bhaskarananda, S. (1998). *The essentials of Hinduism*. Sri Ramakrishna Math Printing Press.

Clark, M. (2002). *Saskatoon community service village: A co-location case study*. Muttart Foundation.

Gardner, H. (2006). *Changing minds: The art and science of changing our own and other peoples minds*. Harvard Business Review Press.

Hawley, J. (1993). *Reawakening the spirit in work: The power of dharmic management*. Berrett-Koehler Publishers.

Olivelle, P. (2006). *The five discourses on worldly wisdom*. NYU Press.

Pham, A., Kalagnanam, S., & Findlay, I. (2020). *Prairie Hospice Society: Social return on analysis report*. Retrieved from Saskatoon.

Sankar, A. (2015). *Environmental management*. Oxford University Press.

Simons, R. (1994). How new top managers use control systems as levers of strategic renewal. *Strategic Management Journal, 15*(3), 169–189.

CHAPTER 9

Concluding Thoughts

9.1 Advice for Rama

Some five to six thousand years ago, there lived a prince named Rama in the kingdom of Ayodhya. Rama's father, King Dasharatha, had three wives—Kausalya, Sumitra, and Kaikeyi. Rama was born to the first queen, Kausalya, and was the eldest of the four sons of Dasharatha. Bharata, Lakshmana, and Shatrugna were his half-brothers. All the brothers were married and were happy in their respective lives. Rama had been married to Sita for twelve years, but the couple enjoyed each other's company with an intensity as if they were married yesterday.

The four brothers were virtuous individuals, and the citizens of Ayodhya loved them all. However, Rama occupied a special place in everybody's hearts. He was an extraordinary human being, who was the epitome of all the dharmic qualities we listed in Chapter 4. In addition, he was extremely handsome, strong, wise, brave, and highly skilled in matters of politics and warfare. If any person was deserving of succeeding Dasharatha, it was Rama.

Dasharatha declared the date of coronation of Rama. The evening before the coronation the entire kingdom was mad with joy that their beloved prince and the most capable and compassionate administrator will be taking over the reins of Ayodhya.

© The Author(s), under exclusive license to Springer Nature Switzerland AG 2022
P. Mishra and S. Kalagnanam, *Managing by Dharma*, Palgrave Studies in Workplace Spirituality and Fulfillment,
https://doi.org/10.1007/978-3-030-90669-6_9

However, fate had different plans. Rama's stepmother, Kaikeyi, who had always been caring and affectionate to Rama got swayed by the wickedness of her maid, Mantharā, and fell into the grips of greed. The evening before the coronation, Kaikeyi invoked a promise that her husband had made to him years ago and used it to fulfill two of her wishes. Her first wish was that her son Bharata—instead of Rama—should be coronated as the king, and her second wish was that Rama be exiled into the forests for fourteen years.

Later that night, when Rama learned about the sudden change of fate, he was shocked beyond belief, but he never lost his dignity. He readily agreed to give up the throne and go away on exile to help maintain the promise of his father. That does not mean that he wasn't hurt by the betrayal of his beloved stepmother. Valmiki, who authored the original Ramayana, writes that Rama couldn't control the tears in his eyes when he went back into his quarters.

He cried the whole night but was fully prepared to proceed on his exile. Rama's wife, Sita, and his brother, Lakshmana, insisted that they will join him on the difficult exile. He went to meet his mother, Kausalya for one last time before his journey. The strong matriarch fainted when she heard the shocking news. She couldn't let her son go on the exile but once she realized the dharmic basis of Rama's decision to go on the exile, she blessed her son with the following words:

Yam palayasi dharmam tvam dhritya cha niyamena cha|
Sa   vai   Raghava-sardula   dharmas-tvam-abhirakshatu|| —   (Valmiki Ramayan, Ayodhya Kandam 25:3)

O Raghava (another name of Rama)! I am unable to do anything to protect you. But the law of dharma is such that it will always protect those who protect it with steadfastness and discipline. Go, continue to live a life committed to dharma.

The story goes that Bharata who was away at the time of these unforeseen developments refused to unfairly take over as Ayodhya's king. Rama, Sita, and Lakshmana, however, continued on their exile to uphold the dharma of keeping one's word. They went through several adventures and misadventures in those fourteen years, but they always conducted themselves as per dharma.

9.2   Dharma's Promise

Life has its ups and downs. Even Rama, the avatar (incarnation) of the Supreme God, Vishnu could not escape the vicissitudes of life. The same was the case with Krishna—Vishnu's later avatar—who also suffered innumerable challenges during his life on Earth. However, both of them weathered the adversities of their respective lives without falling apart.

In our society today, we see innumerable people going into a sinkhole of learned helplessness, anxiety, depression, and committing suicide after facing difficult challenges in their lives (Beiter et al., 2015; Eisenberg et al., 2007; Fernandes et al., 2018; Liu et al., 2019; Mortier et al., 2018). There appears to be a mental health crisis (Evans et al., 2018) in the world, which has been further aggravated by the recent COVID-19 pandemic that has resulted in millions of deaths (Dong & Bouey, 2020).

Starting businesses have always been risky. Approximately 20% of small businesses fail during their first year of operation; this proportion has gone up to 50% in 2020 after the COVID-19 pandemic hit the world (Percentage of businesses that fail). Businessmen go through stages similar to bereavement following such setbacks (Shepherd, 2004).

When misfortune hits good people, it breaks many people apart. "Why bad things happen to good people" (Kushner, 2007) is a longstanding question that has probably bothered humanity from its very inception. Religions try to give hope by promising people that faith in God will help reverse their misfortunes (Koenig, 1994; Snyder et al., 2002).

Dharma makes no such promise. Both the philosophical treatise and the narrative scriptures in the dharmic literature make it explicitly clear that one cannot avoid misfortunes in life—because of the complex ways that karmas work. In other words, dharma may not provide any (false) solace that things will get better. Dharma also does not promise to punish the perpetrators of those who ostensibly caused you misfortune. Such promises, if made, would not only be false but promote magical thinking that may make it even more difficult to bounce back from the adversities.

In the words of Manu, what dharma promises is this:

Dharma eva hato hanti, dharmo raksati raksitah |- Manusmriti, 8.15.

If you destroy dharma, dharma will destroy you. If you protect dharma, dharma will protect you.

You will notice that Manu's words are very similar to what Kausalya blessed Rama with. Both urge us to live our life based on dharma because when we do that dharma will always protect us. What does this promise exactly mean? How will dharma protect its adherent?

Fortune is essentially the advent of artha into our lives, and misfortune is its leaving. As discussed in Chapter 3, dharma is that fundamental purushārtha which aids in the attainment and retainment of the other purushārthas, especially artha and kāma. Thus, dharma protects us through the enhanced physical, psychological, and spiritual capacities that are developed through a commitment to dharma. In the language of modern psychology, a commitment to dharma strengthens certain personality traits of conscientiousness, emotional stability, openness, and internal locus of control which have been found to have a significant positive impact on resilience (Campbell-Sills et al., 2006; Mishra & McDonald, 2017). In the language of the Bhagavad Gita, dharma helps us develop the quality of *sthitaprajnya* (Verses 2.53–55), where our mind is stabilized irrespective of the turmoil around us.

9.3   Final Words

The Hindu religion is the oldest religion that exists today. Referred to as the *Sanātana Dharma* (literally means "eternal principles") by its followers, it is the only surviving pre-Bronze Age civilization. All other civilizations from that period (e.g., the Mesopotamian civilization, the ancient Greek civilization, the ancient Roman civilization, the ancient Egyptian civilization, the Aztecs and Mayan civilizations, and many more) have turned into ashes with the passage of time. This then raises the question, "Is the survival of the Hindu civilization a mere fluke or did the Hindus live by some principles that helped them survive despite a millennium of onslaught that they suffered from outside forces?".

If we have truly understood the true meaning of dharma, then there is no doubt that it is dharma that has helped keep Hinduism alive, even though it has suffered civilizational attacks from other forces for over 1,500 years. Our point is not to gloat over the survival of Hinduism. Rather, our point is that the Hindu religion has survived for such a long time primarily because it has adhered to the foundations of dharma. Once the majority of people within the religion start giving greater importance to artha and kāma than to the foundational purushārtha of dharma, the religion will inevitably get wiped off the face of Earth, as was Rāvana's golden Lankapuri and the many other great civilizations of the past.

Dharma cannot prevent death. Death is inevitable, be it of human beings, organizations, nations, religions, or civilizations. It is emphasized in many places throughout the dhārmic literature that civilizations, planets, universes, and even gods go through death. Thus, there is no reason to fear the death of ourselves, our loved ones, our organizations, our religions, and even our civilizational identities, because death will inevitably happen to all of us. Further, as the Yogasutras of Patānjali says, compulsive clinging to life is a form of klesha (or a cause of suffering), called Abhinivesa. Being living beings, it is natural also for all human beings to enhance our lives and the lives of identities (e.g., our jobs, the business organizations we own) to last forever. However, the compulsive fear of death actually prevents us from living a meaningful life as well as a long life.

"Yato Dharmastato Jaya," says the Brihadaranyaka Upanishad [1:4:14]. The phrase also appears at least eleven different times in the Mahābhārata. The message is "where there is dharma there shall be victory." People often mistranslate the shloka as meaning that good will always prevail over evil. We will not attempt to contradict this opinion, because such interpretations are a matter of personal faith. However, what we can say with confidence is that dharma makes human beings, organizations, countries, and even civilizations stronger. This is how dharma leads to victory.

References

Beiter, R., Nash, R., McCrady, M., Rhoades, D., Linscomb, M., Clarahan, M., & Sammut, S. (2015). The prevalence and correlates of depression, anxiety, and stress in a sample of college students. *Journal of Affective Disorders, 173,* 90–96.

Campbell-Sills, L., Cohan, S. L., & Stein, M. B. (2006). Relationship of resilience to personality, coping, and psychiatric symptoms in young adults. *Behaviour Research and Therapy, 44*(4), 585–599.

Dong, L., & Bouey, J. (2020). Public mental health crisis during COVID-19 pandemic, China. *Emerging Infectious Diseases, 26*(7), 1616.

Eisenberg, D., Gollust, S. E., Golberstein, E., & Hefner, J. L. (2007). Prevalence and correlates of depression, anxiety, and suicidality among university students. *American Journal of Orthopsychiatry, 77*(4), 534–542.

Evans, T. M., Bira, L., Gastelum, J. B., Weiss, L. T., & Vanderford, N. L. (2018). Evidence for a mental health crisis in graduate education. *Nature Biotechnology, 36*(3), 282–284.

Fernandes, M. A., Vieira, F. E. R., Silva, J. S., Avelino, F. V. S. D., & Santos, J. D. M. (2018). Prevalence of anxious and depressive symptoms in college students of a public institution. *Revista Brasileira De Enfermagem, 71*, 2169–2175.

Koenig, H. (1994). Religion and hope. In J. S. Levin (Ed.), *Religion in aging and health: Theoretical foundations and methodological frontiers* (pp. 18–51). Sage.

Kushner, H. S. (2007). *When bad things happen to good people.* Anchor.

Liu, C. H., Stevens, C., Wong, S. H., Yasui, M., & Chen, J. A. (2019). The prevalence and predictors of mental health diagnoses and suicide among US college students: Implications for addressing disparities in service use. *Depression and Anxiety, 36*(1), 8–17.

Mishra, P., & McDonald, K. (2017). Career resilience: An integrated review of the empirical literature. *Human Resource Development Review, 16*(3), 207–234.

Mortier, P., Cuijpers, P., Kiekens, G., Auerbach, R., Demyttenaere, K., Green, J., Kessler, R. C., Nock, M. K., & Bruffaerts, R. (2018). The prevalence of suicidal thoughts and behaviours among college students: A meta-analysis. *Psychological Medicine, 48*(4), 554–565.

Percentage of businesses that fail. https://www.oberlo.com/statistics/percentage-of-businesses-that-fail.

Shepherd, D. A. (2004). Educating entrepreneurship students about emotion and learning from failure. *Academy of Management Learning & Education, 3*(3), 274–287.

Snyder, C. R., Sigmon, D. R., & Feldman, D. B. (2002). Hope for the sacred and vice versa: Positive goal-directed thinking and religion. *Psychological Inquiry, 13*(3), 234–238.

INDEX

Printed in the United States
by Baker & Taylor Publisher Services